G000069124

Madeleine J. CROLL (Mrs.)
Tärnby
8 Woodvale Avenue
Chestfield
Whitstable, Kent
Telephone: Chestfield 2961

A VETERINARY ODYSSEY

A VETERINARY ODYSSEY

Frank H. Manley
M.B.E., D.V.M., M.Sc., M.R.C.V.S.

Best Wishes
Frank

Exposition Press
Hicksville, New York

FIRST EDITION

© 1978 by Frank H. Manley

ISBN 0-682-49115-2

Printed in the United States of America

To my wife, Megan

CONTENTS

A VETERINARY ODYSSEY

1

IN THE BEGINNING

A fresh blanket of snow fresh fallen over sloping fields, gleaming in the morning sun. Clusters of pod-topped weeds woven of bronze, here and there sprinkling the spotless expanse of white. Dark sprays of slender, metallic straight lines, tipped with quivering dots. Pattern to the eye of the sun, as the sun spread delicate networld of more pattern in the blue shadows of the white beneath.

"Come, my boy," said Uncle John to his sister Anna's nine-year-old. "Come now and I will show you how to go." Taking the boy by the hand he pulled his big hat down over his shock of grey hair and started across and up the sloping field toward a point upon which he had fixed his keen blue eyes. Neither to the right nor to the left, intent upon his goal, straight forward he walked, possessed.

But soon the boy caught the play of naked weed against the snow—sharp shadows laced in the blue arabesque beneath. Leaving his mitten in the strong grasp he got free. He ran first to the left to gather beads on stems, then beads on tassels on more stems. Then right on to gather prettier ones, again left to some darker and more brilliant, and beyond to a low spreading kind. Farther on again to tall golden lines, tipped with delicate clusters of dark bronze heads. Eager, trembling, to and fro he ran.

A long way up the slope, arriving at the point on which he had fixed, Uncle John turned to look back. A smile of satisfaction lit the strong Welsh face. His tracks in the snow were straight as any string could be straight. The boy came up, arms full, face flushed, face glowing. He looked up at his uncle—see what he had found. A stern look came down on him. The lesson was to come. Back there was the long, straight, mindful, heedless line

11

*Uncle John's own feet had purposefully made. He pointed to it
with pride. And there was the wavering, searching, heedful line
embroidering the straight one like some free, engaging vine as
it ran back and forth across it. He pointed to that with gentle
reproof. Both stood back. The small hand with the half-frozen
fingers was again in its mitten in the older, stronger hand; an
indulgent benevolent smile down now on the shamed young face.
And somehow there was something not clear.*

*Uncle John's meaning was plain . . . "Neither to the right nor
to the left, but straight is the way."*

*The boy looked at his treasure and then at his Uncle John's
pride, comprehending more than Uncle John meant that he
should. The boy was troubled. Uncle John had left something
out that made all the difference. . . ."*

From *The Autobiography of
Frank Lloyd Wright*

I was born in 1900 in the village of Cefn Mawr in North
Wales close to the English border. In English the name means
"Big Back." A free translation would be "the big hill." My father
was English, born in the adjacent county of Cheshire. Apart
from Cefn itself, which was a typical mining village, this was and
still is a beautiful countryside. My father was a draughtsman at
the Ruabon brickworks. At one time this brick was famous
throughout Britain. I believe my father started work by pushing
a wheelbarrow at the same works. He became an architectural
draughtsman and one time when we were living in New York he
worked on the plans of the Woolworth Building, then the tallest
building in the world. I well remember seeing some of the drawings.

Some years ago, seeking signs of my ancestors, we visited the
village of Manley in Cheshire. We called at the manor house and
a mature gentleman came to the door. It was the grandson of the
famous prime minister, Gladstone. He said that the Manleys were
no longer living in the village. I have yet to find how the village
got its name.

Years later, through the Linfords of Tamworth, long-time

friends whom my wife had met in her singing days, we located
a small old parish church at Weeford in Staffordshire, where many
of the Manleys were buried—apparently not without honor. They
were a military family. One of the stained glass windows in the
church had been "stolen" from France!

My travels started at an early age. When I was eight years
old I was taken by my parents from our small Welsh village to
New York. I do not remember seeing a car before leaving. Those
were the days of the horse and trap, very pleasant in summer
but bitterly cold in the winter. At one time my cousin and I would
drive three or four miles at dawn to pick up milk from another
farm. I remember trips in a canal boat pulled by a horse over a
bridge called the Aqueduct through the beautiful village of
Llangollen, where the international eisteddfod is now held an-
nually. Many of the roads and fine bridges of that time were
designed by a famous engineer named Thomas Telford. In those
days my father, like many middle class people, owned a bicycle
on which he took long rides over the countryside. The roads were
not paved and tire punctures were common. A few years later
we all were to repeat similar experiences with cars. I also remember my Grandfather Jones, a large man with a long beard. Every
Saturday the grandchildren appeared before him to receive six-
pence each. I still think of him as my idea of Moses. Perhaps
this was due to the Semitic cast to his features, most notably a
long beard and a prominent nose.

I have been lucky in that I have been in places where interesting and sometimes dramatic events were taking place, for
example, in Uganda in the days of the protectorate; in Cyprus
during the 1932 disturbances; in Israel during the 1952 war; in
London on V-E Day; and in Rhodesia soon after the 1966
unilateral declaration of independence.

My father had already left for New York early in 1908 and
a few months later my mother, my sister, Beryl, and I sailed
from Liverpool on the White Star ship, the *Celtic*. Because my
father was already in the country we were spared the rigors of
Ellis Island, where many immigrants were held for examination.
We went to live on Staten Island—a suburban area. We were

struck by the fact that the houses were made of wood, as we had never seen that before. The weather took on a different rhythm with long hot summers and cold winters with plenty of snow and ice. One winter for several weeks we children skated to school. We lived in Tottenville at the extreme tip of the Island, and I attended Public School Number One and later Curtis High School. When the time came for me to study French, I had to transfer to a private school. German was the common second language in the high schools at that time. I was usually an A student. I mention this because when I eventually returned to England, I found myself at least a year behind academically.

We first lived in a small flat, also something new to us, but soon moved to a two-story house complete with a porch and basement. It had a nice garden with fruit trees and, of all things, a grape arbor. This was a happy time for my parents. Here my sister Myra was born. She is now living in Spain. Because of its warm climate and low cost of living, Spain became a haven for Britishers in the sixties and seventies.

The automobile was now a common sight. There was even an occasional steam car. For a football game at Princeton quite a number of cars would pass our house en route from New York. At that time there was no bridge to Jersey, and one crossed the Staten Island Sound on the Amboy ferry.

Once a week my father and I would walk down town to the Chinese laundry. The men still wore pigtails, a Chinese custom in those days.

One day we visited some open fields to see two Frenchmen try to fly a biplane. It only managed to rise in the air a few feet, something far removed from the modern jet! Years later Megan and I were passengers on one of the first flights in the British Comet, the first commercial jet plane; but somehow those first flying pioneers seemed more daring. Certainly there were fewer people in the team.

The summers on the Island were pleasant for youngsters with lots of swimming, since we lived within walking distance of the beach. In the evening the grown-ups sat on the porch, although mosquitoes were often a nuisance. Those from nearby New

Jersey had the reputation of being the biggest. The baseball team from over there was called the "Jersey Skeeters." Almost every evening our gang of boys would walk down to the railway station to get the late newspaper from New York, which contained the latest baseball results. I remember my father once taking me to the city to see the New York Giants play. And another time he took me to Madison Square Garden to see the Buffalo Bill Wild West Show. The Indian chief in the show was Sitting Bull. Of course, I knew little about politics at that time but I remember a great outcry when Rockfeller raised the price of kerosene by a fraction of a cent—shades of the modern fuel crisis!

My uncle, Professor Share Jones, then the dean of the Veterinary School at Liverpool University, persuaded my parents to send me to England to finish my education. In 1916, in the middle of the First World War, I left New York. Off the coast of Ireland we were attacked by a German submarine. The captain of our ship ordered full speed astern. Fortunately, we were not damaged, but traveling by sea then was a dangerous business. It was even worse during the Second World War.

I went to live with my uncle in North Wales. It must have seemed a bit odd to see a youngster arriving from the States in the middle of a war. I was a bit young to enter the university and in any case did not have the necessary credits, so it was decided that private study was the thing. It is not to be recommended from my experience. The companionship of school friends and school sports are missed. I had played with the baseball and basketball teams in high school in New York, and I missed it. I did, however, eventually matriculate. There were very few veterinary students at Liverpool at that time. Even so, dormitory room was limited and I lived either in lodgings or in North Wales on my uncle's farm. The latter entailed two hours commuting every day and occasionally a two-mile walk from the main line junction. This was sometimes enlivened by the company of a pretty lady dental student. Military conscription was then in force and after a spell in the Officers Training Corps, I was in the Royal Marine Submarine Miners. They had control of mine fields around the coasts of Belgium and Britain. It only lasted a few months for me—the war was over and students were allowed to return immediately to resume their studies. I had been in Liverpool when the first "Doughboys" arrived and, many years later after the Second World War, was the veterinary officer in Southampton when the G.I.s were shipping home on the *Queen Mary* and other ships.

The Veterinary School at Liverpool University was then a controversial one. It was the first in Great Britain to be an integral part of a university and the first in Britain to award a degree in Veterinary Science, in contrast to the diploma of the Royal College of Veterinary Surgeons, which was awarded by the governing body of that college. The Liverpool School of Tropical Medicine, where I took several courses, had a romantic association with the early work then being carried out on tropical diseases—particularly that being carried out in West and East Africa on malaria. The names of Newstead, Yorke and Blacklock were famous. Strange that a few years later I found myself working with an International Sleeping Sickness Commission in Uganda. All the examiners of the Royal College were external examiners, so that the students were not examined by their own teachers. Although the student body was small, it was an interesting group. The first lady student of all time at the college was Miss Knight. She married a fellow student, Dr. Taylor, who was to become the parasitologist at the veterinary laboratory of the Ministry of Agriculture at Weybridge. He became well known for his philosophical manner of writing about parasites—not an easy task. Tom Hare, another student, was president of the Students' Union and was perhaps the first to take degrees in Medicine and Veterinary Science at the same time. Holly Thornton was a star of the rugby team and then for many years chief meat inspector in Newcastle-on-Tyne. Much later he became advisor to the rebel Rhodesian government, and there we met again when, in 1966, I went out there as microbiologist.

Upon my graduation it was decided that I should practice in North Wales. It was not a great success. One of the reasons that might seem strange now was that I could not speak Welsh and the farmers could not speak English. The coming of the radio was one of the reasons that the English language began to permeate the countryside. Welsh and English are taught in all Welsh schools now. I decided that I would soon have to make a change. The first step was to complete the degree of Bachelor of Veterinary Science at Liverpool University. This I did in 1924, perhaps only the second person to receive this degree. The degree was presented by Lord Derby, the vice chancellor of the university, who remarked that it was good to see students taking degrees in Veterinary Science. Soon all the veterinary schools in Great Britain were integral parts of the universities, and a good percentage of the students were taking degrees.

2

UGANDA

In 1925 I applied for an appointment in the Colonial Office and was interviewed by Major Furse. Over the years he interviewed hundreds of men who served in the colonies. It was a very informal sort of thing, and there was very little red tape. A few weeks after the interview I was offered an appointment in Uganda. Faced with reality I must confess to some periods of doubt and "butterflies in the stomach." Uganda seemed a long way off in those days. The Colonial Office sent me the *Uganda Handbook,* which was dated 1920. Reading this was presumably equal to a modern briefing or indoctrination. There was a lot of information about what to eat, what to wear, what equipment was necessary, and the health conditions in the country. Much of the advice now seems strange. One had to wear a hat at all times when in the sun, preferably a double terai or pith helmet, which should be lined with red silk; also, when on safari, one had to wear a spine pad. This was a pad of cloth, again lined with red silk, which could be buttoned to the back of the shirt—presumably to protect the spine from the rays of the sun. A good bit of advice was to boil and filter all water before drinking it. This was a very wise precaution against bacterial and parasitic diseases. Knee-length mosquito boots had to be worn at night as a precaution against mosquito bites, since in many areas malaria was very prevalent. In fact, most people took five grains of quinine daily.

In those days it took a month to make the journey from London to Mombasa. We sailed from Tilbury docks on a British India line ship of about 8,000 tons, and after the usual rather rough trip through the Bay of Biscay, called at Marseilles. My cabin colleagues were a young doctor going to Zanzibar and a surveyor going to what was then Tanganyika. We went ashore in the evening, but as we were later heading back along the docks we were stopped by the police, who suggested that it might be safer if we took a taxi. Prevention is better than a cure!

At Port Said the usual small boats came alongside, their owners selling all kinds of Egyptian ware, and there was the famous gulli gulli man with his conjuring tricks. We then entered the Suez Canal, and what a fascinating experience that was. The next port was Port Sudan. Again we were able to get ashore and walk around the town. We were now in a new world with all the atmosphere of the East. We were in a country of cloudless blue skies and dazzling white buildings. I hardly thought that in a few weeks I would be on safari in the West Nile Province near the Sudan border and in the middle of the African bush. Like all ships then, we put in for coal in Aden. We went ashore and, according to the custom of those days, climbed the hill above the town to the wells. We threw stones down the wells to test the great depths. Also according to custom, I went to an Indian fortune-teller. I do not remember what he told me so it probably was not very interesting. We turned the Cape of Good Hope and headed south along the east coast. It was hot and humid. We were becoming excited with the thought that in a few days we would be in Mombasa. There we had to wait a day for the train to Nairobi. That evening I went ashore with one of the old-timers who took me to a nearby village. This was my first look at the real Africa, and we even saw some dancing. Here I was to experience for the first time the sound of the African drums— a sound that is so linked with the African bush. While crossing a road one day, I distinctly heard the voice of Megan, who was of course far away in Wales. It was a very small thing, but strangely enough I have never forgotten it. Later she came out and we were married in Mombasa Cathedral.

The train to Uganda was delayed in Nairobi for two days, so I took this opportunity to visit the veterinary department in Kabete, hardly thinking that forty-five years later I would be in the British Voluntary Service and would be teaching there.

The laboratory was already well known for its work on tropical veterinary medicine. The chief veterinary officer was an Irishman, Colonel Doherty. He informed me that the judge for the Nairobi race meeting was sick and that he would like me to take his place. I did so with some misgivings; although I was a good horseman, my only connection with the racetrack had been watching the famous Grand National at Aintree when I was a student at Liverpool. Fortunately there were no problems. Forty years later I was the veterinary officer to the Turf Club in Rhodesia.

The railway did not go all the way to Uganda but rather stopped at the port of Kisumu on Lake Victoria. The ships were small paddle steamers with a few cabins on the deck. It was an overnight journey to Port Bell—the Ugandan port near the capital city of Kampala. Swarms of lake flies swept across the lake from time to time, but they were quite harmless. However, mosquito nets over the bed were now a must. Uganda is a lofty plateau in the heart of tropical Africa, 500 miles from the nearest seashore. It is a country of strange and beautiful contrasts. Winston Churchill, after his visit in 1908 had this to say about Uganda: "The forests of Uganda, for magnificence, for variety of form, for profusion of brilliant life, plant, bird, insect, reptile, beast, for the vast scale and awful fecundity of the natural processes that are beheld at work, eclipsed and indeed effaced all previous impressions." Of the source of the Nile he said, "Jinja is destined to become a very important place in the economy of Central Africa. In years to come the shores of this splendid bay may be crowned with villas and imposing offices, and the gorge of the Nile crowded with factories and warehouses. There is power enough. . ." At nearby Murchison Falls there is now a dam and large power plant.

In June, 1877 the first two Europeans to settle in Uganda—Lieut. Shergold Smith, R.N., and the Reverend R. T. Wilson—arrived in Rubaga, the court of the then king of Uganda, Mutesa I. In 1882 the first five converts of the mission were baptized and the Anglican church of Uganda came into being. Smith and a companion had been murdered at the south end of the lake, but shortly afterwards a number of other missionaries arrived.

The Christian missions introduced the first industrial work, carpentering, brick making, printing, and the cultivation of coffee and other products. Through mission efforts the language was first reduced to writing and the first medical service introduced.

After arriving in Kampala I spent a few days at the veterinary headquarters, getting camping equipment, stores and servants, since I was being posted to Arua in the West Nile Province. This was considered a remote area in those days. I also needed a motorbike.

The journey entailed traveling by truck to Jinja, by train to Namasagali in the middle of the flat, hot Eastern Province, and then by another truck to Masindi. There I stayed in the government rest house for the night. In the morning there was another truck ride to Busia on Lake Albert. After Jinja there were no paved roads. At Busia we boarded a small paddle steamer and headed across the lake and down the Nile to Rhino camp. We made two stops at riverside villages. This was an unforgettable experience, particularly since part of the trip was during the night. I still remember the blackness and stillness, the former broken by the light of bush fires in the distance and the latter by the cries of big game. Hippos and crocodiles abounded on the river banks, many swimming in the river much of the time. Except for the captain of the little steamer I was the only white person on board. At Rhino camp I was met by the district commissioner from Arua. We had traveled a few miles in his car when we had to stop by a small pool to fill the radiator with water. We were both standing in the middle of the road when a lion crossed about fifty yards away. It was a nice introduction to the African bush, and I felt that I now was really on my way. Game parks were practically nonexistent at the time. There were no paved roads in the province; in fact, there were very few roads of any kind.

The West Nile was not only the most inaccessible part of Uganda but the tribes there were perhaps the most primitive, except for the Pygmies of the Western Province, whom I later met near the Mountains on the Moon. The West Nile was incorporated into Uganda in 1914. Prior to that, Belgium exercised some in-

fluence over the area. Of the many tribes the Alur and the Lug-
bara were the largest, both with a strong Nilotic strain, particularly,
of course, near the Nile river. There was little cohesion among
the tribes, the principal units being the family and the clan. When
I was there the mode of life was very simple. Only grass huts
existed. Very little clothing was worn. The men wore animal
skins draped from the shoulder, if anything. Women wore a
pubic plug and a sort of brush between the buttocks made of
banana leaves.

There was no artificial light of course. The natives were up
at dawn: the men to look after the cattle, repair the huts, and
perhaps till the fields; the women to prepare the food, carry wood
and water, and feed the babies. The babies here are breast fed
for much longer than white babies. The main crops were maize,
millet, beans, and cassava. Cattle were and of course still are a
sign of wealth. Cotton and coffee were subsequently introduced
as cash crops. There was little in the way of artificial amusement
except hunting, beer parties, and dancing, which the African loves.

My main job concerned the control of rinderpest—a disease
of cattle and other ruminants caused by a virus and one of the
most devastating diseases in Africa at that time. This meant a
walking safari, which took me north nearly to the Sudan border.
I had my motorbike with me, but most of the time it was pushed
along narrow tracks or had to be carried across shallow rivers.
Camping and veterinary equipment was carried by thirty porters.
Usually I and my personal servant, Israeli, walked at the head
of the column. I carried one of my Manlichner-Schoener rifles, and
Israeli, my aide, proudly carried my Webly revolver. I joined
up with a stock inspector in the field. We each had our own
tents for sleeping and during the day shared a grass *banda*.
Before treating the cattle, my first job was to establish good
relations with the local chief. Without this relationship the work
would become very difficult. A kraal was made and instructions
given for several hundred cattle to be brought in every morning
at sunrise. The animals were thrown down in long rows in the
kraal, three tribesmen being assigned to each animal. The inoculation then consisted of an injection of virus from a naturally or

artificially infected animal. At the same time immune serum was injected. This was obtained from a recently recovered animal, whose blood was collected in glass jars. After the clot had formed, a weight was lowered in each jar, which caused the serum to rise to the top from where it was drawn off. As much sterility as possible was used and it seemed to work remarkably well. A mistake made in the early days was in not making absolutely sure that the virus was free from piroplasms—a blood parasite. Later we made sure of this by adding a solution of tartar emetic. This was most effective.

The kraal activity was hot, dusty, and noisy. Inevitably one or two of the cattle would cut loose and this often led to a mad stampede. This was the part that the tribesmen loved. They were for the most part tall and strong due to their Nilotic ancestry, and it was exciting to see them chasing and throwing these very wild animals.

For the men clothing and material possessions were very few. The camps were primitive too. During the heat of the day we remained in our mud and wattle building. This had open sides so that we had the benefit of the breeze in the afternoon. But we were not without comforts. At camp we received our mail by runner. He carried the letters in a cleft stick. And speaking of mail, the famous letter sent by H. M. Stanley to the *Daily Telegraph* in 1875—appealing for missionaries to be sent to Uganda—took seven months to get to England. Today, thanks to the jet, a letter posted in Kampala one day can be in London the next.

Every day the chief and some of his men would pay a visit and often brought us eggs and chickens. The eggs were very small and cost one shilling for fifty. Sometimes these were given as presents. In fact on all my safaris in the African bush, I was always received with kindness. Going to one camp I and some of my safari became lost and walked twenty-five miles before we got to our destination. That same night we experienced a terrific thunderstorm. I was in bed when the tent was blown down and a herd of cattle stampeded through the camp. On going to another camp and for some reason not making it before dark, we had to pitch camp under the stars. Anyone who has had this experience out in the African countryside will know how beautiful it is. There is nothing quite like it and the charm is enhanced by the near presence of big game.

After a very successful inoculation campaign I returned to Arua. There were only five white people on the station. There was a medical officer and a hospital of sorts, but I think most of the government men were usually on safari. I soon received orders to leave the West Nile Province and to proceed to Entebbe for duty in the laboratory. This suited me very well. Before leaving I managed a trip to Aru in the Congo on my motorbike. The veterinary officer there was doing the human medicine in the absence of a medical officer.

The journey from Arua to Entebbe provided some interesting adventures. My camping equipment and staff went on ahead of me by truck. We were to catch the paddle steamer from Rhino camp the next morning. I traveled on my motorbike and it was getting near dusk when I was still some distance from the Nile. A heavy thunderstorm suddenly came up. Riding on the dirt road became difficult and the bike finally broke down. I pushed it along for a mile or so but then had to leave it at the side of the road and walk on. By now it was quite dark. I knew that I was in big game country and began to look for a suitable tree in which I could spend the night. Suddenly there appeared the lights of a car heading toward me. The truck pulled up. The driver, who was carrying a rifle on the front seat, said, "I nearly shot you. The last thing I expected to see on this road at night was a walking man. You are about three miles from Rhino camp. Take one of my servants with a safari lamp. You will be all right." I was very wet and tired when I did arrive in camp. The next morning my bike was brought in.

We then boarded the paddle steamer for Butiaba on Lake Albert. It was the captain's first trip. There were three other passengers. After about two hours sailing we became stuck in the Sudd. This is a mass of papyrus grass that floats in the river. We were stuck there for two days. An Australian prospector and I somehow managed to get ashore with our rifles and enjoyed some tracking in what was surely virgin bush, and it was a very pleasant experience. We were taken off in a large launch and headed for Butiaba. Before we reached there a nasty storm arose and things were unpleasant for an hour or so. I remember lying on the deck and rolling from one side of the launch to the other. At Butiaba we were picked up by truck transport and reached Kampala and then Entebbe without further incident. The equipment and staff arrived a few days later.

Entebbe was of course a very pleasant station in those days. It was the center of the British administration, which consisted of the governor and the Legislative Council. This consisted at first of white civil servants. As time went on, Black and Asian representatives were included. The headquarters of the African government of Buganda was in Kampala. The ruler was the *kabaka*. There was a Parliament or Lukiko but most of the members were appointed by the kabaka. Each province of the protectorate had a somewhat similar administration. The British officials—such as the district commissioners, the medical officers, district engineers, veterinary officers, and others were appointed by the Colonial Office and served under the governor.

But back to Entebbe. It has a well nigh perfect climate. The veterinary laboratory staff shared a building on the lakeshore with the International Sleeping Sickness Commission. We had doctors from France, Germany, Portugal, and Britain. I had the pleasure of working with them on a number of projects. Some time prior to this, in an attempt to control the sleeping sickness that had devastated the area, the lakeshore and the Sesse Islands had been depopulated of man and animals. Now on an experimental basis they were being returned, and it was our job to test the blood for reinfection. We made many trips to the islands. One time I went over in a canoe manned by twenty native oarsmen.

The *Handbook of Uganda,* 1920, reported that as a result of stringent sleeping sickness regulations, the islands in Lake Victoria and the foreshores of lakes and rivers had been evacuated, except at recognized points that were kept clear of vegetation favored by the tsetse fly—the carrier of the causal blood parasite.

The prohibited area had been reduced to one mile in the case of
Lake Victoria, and investigations were being carried out with a
view to early repopulation in other areas of Buganda. Sometimes
I went over to the islands on a small steam launch. On the evening
of sailing my servant would put up my bed complete with
mosquito net on the small deck. I was of course the only white
passenger. The nights were warm and tropical and it was a
pleasant and peaceful way to cross the lake. I used to stay at a
rest house and once walked across one of the larger islands to
catch a native canoe to Bukakata on the mainland. Most of the
Sesses are beautifully green and some are covered with dense
forest.

After six months I was transferred to Fort Portal in the
Western Province. This was considered the healthiest part of the
protectorate. The station was 4,000 feet above sea level and
practically free from the anophelese mosquito. My house was a
delightful if rather primitive mud and wattle bungalow with a
magnificent view of the snow-capped Ruwenzori mountain range—
the fabled Mountains of the Moon. One of my duties was to
investigate the reported smuggling of hides and skins across
the Congo border. This meant a walking safari with Pygmy porters
and a scrambling descent down 2,000 feet of escarpment. At
the bottom there was a rest camp. Here my tent was pitched
and I spent the night. During the afternoon another safari came
in. This consisted of a white hunter and a honeymoon couple
just out from Paris. I thought it a bit unusual that while the
young husband went out looking for buffalo, the white hunter
stayed in camp and entertained the bride without considering
too much that I was in a nearby tent. I wonder if young people
today, so conscious of their desire for all kinds of freedom,
realize that perhaps things in some ways do not change that
much. . . .

The next morning I headed for the Semliki camp, which
was right on the banks of the river Semliki. The plain was at that
time teeming with game, and the river with crocodiles and hippos.
The following day I met the local chief, and we discussed how
he could stop the bringing of hides across the border and pointed

out the danger of the spread of infectious diseases. The game here had rarely been shot at and seemed to be quite unafraid. I shot two impalas, as we were getting short of food. Later in the same area I shot a buffalo. This was an interesting hunt through some elephant grass, some of which had been burnt. The buffalo is, of course, considered to be the most dangerous animal of all. I used by Manlicher-Schoener .375. Although I was in range of big game on many occasions, I did very little shooting except when we were without food.

After returning to Fort Portal, I applied for leave to go to Mombasa to meet my fiancée, who was then on the way out from Wales. We were married in Mombasa Cathedral. Nearly fifty years later when I was working with the British Voluntary Service in Kenya, we visited the cathedral on a number of occasions. We checked some of the old church books to see if our names were still there. They were.

We were looking forward to our tour in the Western Province very much—but it was not to be. At Kampala I was informed that I was being transferred to the Eastern Province. This was disappointing; furthermore, the Eastern Province had the reputation of having a high incidence of malaria. After a few weeks in Jinja I was to be the veterinary officer in Mbale, which was situated at the foot of Mount Elgon. By this time I had bought a secondhand Chevrolet. Like most cars of that time it was an open model. For a long time we were without a cap on the radiator and used to stuff a potato in the hole. From time to time when the water boiled up the potato was blown out. This happened quite often with the old cars. In Jinja we used to have picnics at the Ripon Falls near the shores of Lake Victoria. This was long before the dam was built nearby. Sir Winston Churchill observed the great potential of the area when he made his visit in 1908.

For the first few days in Jinja there was no housing available, so we had to pitch tent in the hotel grounds. One night Megan and I, with a few other guests armed only with safari lamps, spent some time chasing hippos back into the lake. No one seemed to realize the possibility of any danger. The hotel was built close to the lakeshore, which, no doubt, was land the hippos considered to be *their* property. We were in Jinja when Sir Alan Cobham landed on the lake in a seaplane, much to the delight of the Africans who rushed to the shore. This was the time of the inauguration of the London to Capetown route across Africa.

One morning we were aroused from bed by Dr. G. Norman Hall, who was then acting as veterinary pathologist in Entebbe. He wanted us to go with him to the island of Buvuma to make some investigations into the incidence of trypanosomaisis. We had very little camping equipment with us, and Megan and I pitched our camp beds out in the open. By then Buvuma was being repopulated. There were guards and other people about, and it was the first time that Megan had undressed under these circumstances. As usual when there was no medical officer available we had to treat some of the natives. We limited our activities to the administration of quinine, aspirin, and castor oil. Soon after this trip I took up my duties as veterinary officer at Mbale, the capital of the Bukedi district.

Mbale was a typical administrative township of the time. There were five bungalows for the European staff made up usually of the district commissioner, the treasurer, medical officer, veterinary officer, agricultural officer, and engineer. Sometimes there were assistants to these jobs, and one or two European nurses. At Mbale we had a very small hospital. The outside was constructed of corrugated iron. It was still there when we returned for a visit in 1957. The roads in the Eastern Province were all of dirt, but because of the nature of the soil they were considered to be quite good—this in spite of the swampy nature of the terrain. Much of the swamp area was filled with papyrus grass or sudd.

Soon after my arrival in the district, an outbreak of rinderpest occurred on the Kenya-Uganda border. Rinderpest as previously indicated is a viral disease that is transmitted directly and indirectly from animal to animal. I decided to set up an inoculation center at Kalait—a rest camp right on the border. There was nothing much at Kalait except a mud and wattle rest house and some huts for the staff. There was a native village a couple of miles away, and the township of Tororo was about twenty miles. It was, of course, very primitive, but it had the blessing of being free from the malaria-carrying mosquito. It was on a slight hill overlooking the surrounding country. The first night we heard a lion roaring in the distance, but he stayed away from the camp. We had plenty of hyenas around, and leopard footprints were found around the tent on several mornings.

Megan and I slept in the tent and spent the day in the rest house. We had the usual two camp chairs, and for our guests we made a seat by removing the car seat and putting it on two petrol cans. The kralls were built and here cattle were brought in to be inoculated with rinderpest virus and serum—in much the same way as we had operated in the West Nile Province. Many of the cattle were heavily infected and although the dose of serum was often increased above normal, the mortality rate was often higher than we liked. We had police guard posts along the Kenya border every half mile or so in an attempt to stop people from transmitting the disease indirectly by moving meat or other products across the border. In those days it was the custom to let the local chiefs deal with minor crime. One day a woman was brought in for smuggling meat. I told the chief to deal with her. The usual punishment for this kind of thing was three strokes on the bottom with a cane. I do not think that Megan ever forgave me for permitting it.

About twenty miles into Kenya was a cotton ginnery managed by a young Englishman called Dans. Every weekend he would come over to our camp on his motorbike and sidecar, complete with ukulele and pet monkey. Dans slept on the car seat in the rest house, but none of us were in isolated luxury. There were a great many rats around the camp and at night they used to run up between the outer fly and the tent proper, so that apart from my rifle I always kept a strong stick by the bedside and from time to time gave the roof of the tent a blow to keep the rats moving. We had very few human visitors at the camp. One day Dans arrived about dawn and told us that a woman at the mission station was expecting a baby and was urgently in need of a doctor. He was on the way to Tororo to get Dr. Mc.Lain.

They arrived back in about an hour and Megan was taken along as a nurse. It was a pretty rough trip. Unfortunately the baby was stillborn. Megan was told to take the baby and to try to get some life into it but to no avail. As Megan was quite pregnant herself and had no experience in nursing, I do not think she enjoyed the occasion. This lady was the only woman Megan saw during our ten weeks in Kalait.

It was now time to get back to our headquarters in Mbale. There were usually only three or four white people on the station, rarely more than three ladies at one time. The district commissioner was an ex-naval officer who had left the service because he could not overcome seasickness! We were lucky in that the wife of the medical officer was also a doctor who was able to take care of my wife. Our daughter became the first white baby to be christened in Mbale. Before the baby, Joan, was born, I was often away from the station. My wife was quite touched when at night she would find one of the servants lying, on guard, on the floor outside the bedroom door.

We now proceeded on leave, this time via Tororo because a branch of the railway had now reached this point en route to Kampala. We stopped the first night at the house of the medical officer in Tororo. This was the same doctor that Megan had previously assisted. He had a serval cat that came in every night for dinner. Much to our chagrin, the cat was always served first! We were nearly persuaded to take it along with us to England. At Mombasa we said good-bye to Israeli, who had been with me since my arrival in Kampala. He was a Baganda, not a big man but very capable of taking charge of a safari no matter how big the porters were. He was a good chap but a bit difficult on pay-day, when we had some stormy sessions. On these occasions I often told him to go. He would go to Megan, the Memsahib, and say, "He does not mean it." He was right.

We were to visit Uganda again in 1957 when I was working in Ethiopia with the American A.I.D. program. Independence was growing close at that time. Complex negotiations were taking place. Milton Apolo Obote, a teacher from Lango in the north, put together a loose national political party that won the last preindependence election in 1962. In 1966 Obote called in the army headed by the rough and ready Idi Amin. The army took over power and the last kabaka or king fled to England. The Buganda were not happy about the loss of their kingdom and power.

Obote was deposed by Amin. The latter has made no concessions to the Buganda but rather has expanded the army and has strengthened the West Nile faction. This is the part of the country from where Amin comes. The future of Uganda seems very difficult with its people deeply divided, the economy in bad shape, and a military dictatorship in power.

3

NIGERIA

I spent several weeks at the veterinary laboratory of the Ministry of Agriculture at Weybridge near London brushing up on techniques and general laboratory diagnostic methods. I was keen on laboratory work and had been appointed veterinary pathologist in Nigeria. While at the laboratory we stayed at the old Dukes Head Hotel—a typical English pub complete with bowling green. This was a game we were to take up later in the Middle East and Africa. The staff at the laboratory was then very small. There were at most four qualified veterinarians. My particular friend there was Jimmy Doyle. He remained there for most of his professional career and became world famous for the diagnosis of Newcastle disease in poultry—a disease that is still of great importance.

I was not allowed to take my wife and child with me to Nigeria because of unknown health conditions in the north, and so I was asked to look the situation over for six months. I sailed from Liverpool on a ship called the *Abinsi* of the Elder Dempster Line. There were only a few passengers. It was of about 3,000 tons and never seemed to stop rolling, although we encountered no really rough seas. The voyage to Lagos took about ten days.

Three centuries ago Nigeria exemplified African civilization. The North was associated with the migration from the Sudan and the South with the city states scattered in West Africa. The French penetrated west from Dakar in the northwest, and the British from the river inlets on the West Coast. The population in West Africa was much denser than in East Africa, and its culture more developed in some ways.

One of the early British explorers was Dr. Backie—a naval officer born in the Orkney Islands. In 1854 he established a government post 350 miles up the river. He was ruler, priest, physician, and schoolmaster. He translated part of the Bible into Hausa—one of the predominant languages. But as in other parts of Africa the missionaries were among the earliest white people to enter tropical Africa. For example, the Moravians formed a mission in the Gold Coast in 1736.

Commercial companies undertook exploration in Nigeria and eventually the United African Company became dominant. Lagos was annexed by the British in 1896. The French and British were dividing West Africa according to their spheres of influence. The colony of Nigeria was divided roughly into three areas. The North was linked with Muslim North Africa and separated from the South by dense forest areas and the Niger and Benue rivers. The people were mostly Hausa and Fulani. The West was inhabited by the organized and culturally advanced Yoruba, and the East by the alert and expanding Ibo. Overall, there is a great diversity of ethnic and linguistic groups.

In 1928 when I arrived in Nigeria, there was a train—complete with sleeping berths—from Lagos to the North. I had brought a car out—a Morris Oxford. I arrived in Vom station to find Ford, the senior laboratory assistant, meeting me. We were both pleased when the car first started to go. There were no paved roads in Northern Nigeria then but a car could still be useful at least in the dry season. Vom was on the Bauchi Plateau, and it was here where the veterinary laboratory and stock farm were located.

There was nothing else there except a native village and, five miles away, a leper colony. The plateau was situated at an altitude of 3,000 feet and was considered one of the healthiest parts of the country. It was generally hot and dry and characterized by the Harmattan—high clouds of fine sand that periodically blew across the country from the deserts to the north—and severe tropical storms. The air was so dry that one's skin became charged with electricity, so that the body gave off large sparks when in contact with certain materials. It was so bad some nights that I would throw off the sheets and jump out of bed.

For some time I was the only veterinarian on the station. There were four laboratory assistants and three stock inspectors, one of the latter being housed at the stock farm three miles away.

Just previous to my arrival at the laboratory, O'Brian—one of the veterinarians—was doing a postmortem on a dog when a splinter of bone hit him in the eye. There was then no vaccine available locally so he had to be sent to Paris for the Pasteur series of inoculations. It must have been an anxious trip, which then took over two weeks. He suffered no ill effects.

Many years later I was examining a cow at the veterinary clinic at Auburn University, Alabama, and had occasion to have my hand well in the cow's mouth, thinking there was some problem in that area. Later we found out that the animal was infected with rabies, and I had to decide whether or not to take the twelve inoculations. At that time the vaccine was made from nerve tissue. The shots were painful and sometimes dangerous. Number eight knocked me down and no more were given! The same year one of our senior students died of complications following rabies shots. Later the vaccine was of chick embryo origin and became easier to take.

The Vom laboratory was then only a few years old. At the time of my arrival there was no senior staff available, so I was left in charge. Almost immediately we encountered a severe and widespread outbreak of blackleg in cattle. This disease, which in nonvaccinated stock proves often fatal, is usually of limited distribution and confined to young stock. In Northern Nigeria at that time the disease occurred in epizootic form and struck animals of all ages. Fortunately, Leclainch and Vallé working in France had just developed a formalized vaccine. This is a culture inactivated by the addition of formalin. At the time it was quite new but it proved to be quite successful.

One day we had spruced up the laboratory for the visit of a high-placed official from London. We were in the middle of the yard when a rabid horse staggered in and then dashed off down the road. Our visitor did not stay very long.

Later we had several cases of typhoid fever among the laboratory staff. Remember, this was before the discovery of antibiotics and our nearest doctor was at the leper colony five miles away. We actually started to make some coffins, and I sent frantic telegrams to the governor in Lagos. We were lucky, and fortunately the outbreak soon passed.

The department was now informed by telegram from the governor of the British Cameroons that cattle were dying from a mysterious disease—could a veterinary officer be sent there to investigate? There was no veterinary department in that country. I was available, and, complete with a batch of guinea pigs, I set off for Lagos—there to catch a German cargo vessel for the port of Victoria. This is located in a beautiful tropical bay with the Cameroons Mountains rising steeply in the background to a height of 3,000 feet. About 30 miles off the coast is the island of Fernando Po, on which the Spaniards exiled their political and other prisoners. The island is dominated by a mountain peak rising to 10,000 feet. I was going to the government station at Buea, situated in the mountains beyond Victoria. It was a green and beautiful spot after the desert climate of Northern Nigeria. The average annual rainfall is 300 inches—one of the highest in the world.

I was invited to stay at the farm where the sick cattle were. It was being managed by a German family, and I sensed even then that the home government was being somewhat oppressive. Some of the cows were obviously ill and one was slaughtered. During the postmortem, tubercular lesions were detected. After microscopically confirming the diagnosis, the herd was tested with tuberculin and over 50 percent reacted. This test is based on a skin reaction, which occurs when tuberculin is injected into the skin of an infected animal. Tuberculin is a purified protein derivative from a growth of the organism causing the disease. This outbreak of tuberculosis in cattle was the first to be reported in tropical Africa. It was interesting in that the cattle were of the Swiss Algaur breed, and they had passed the test before being exported from Europe. The conditions under which they were kept were almost ideal in that there was unlimited fresh air, sunshine, and green food. The only bad thing from the point of view of transmission was that when the cows were in the shed they were arranged in two rows facing each other. As this was the first report of the occurrence of the disease in West Africa, on my return to Vom I recommended that the herd be slaughtered as soon as possible.

On my way back to Vom, Megan and my baby daughter, Joan, met me in Lagos. While waiting for the upcountry train, we stayed at the government rest house, which was on the race-course—so we saw little of the town of Lagos. Soon after returning to Vom we acquired two young horses, one of which we entered in the Jos races. Jos was the capital of the province, but we only went there once a week to buy our foodstuffs and other necessities. There were the usual white officials there, but I do not remember any of them. For some reason or other we preferred to keep to Vom. Of course we went to Jos for the races. On one occasion I had an exciting experience. I was asked to ride a horse in the mile and a quarter, which was the big race. The odds against the horse's winning were a hundred to one. But it was a nice looking horse and toward the finish it was going strong with only two horses in front. Then my mount surged forward and went between the other two to finish first. However with the spectators standing on their seats because of the odds, I was hauled before the stewards and disqualified for a technical offense. Apparently my horse had impeded the progress of one of the other horses. This was the first big race in which I had ridden and of course one I never forgot.

Several new houses were now being built near the laboratory, and the staff was increased. G. Norman Hall came out as veterinary pathologist. Norman was a friend we knew in Uganda. We both received degrees from the University of Zurich. Later Norman followed me to Iraq on an assignment for the United Nations. But this was many years in the future. Megan and I were living in one of the old bungalows. It was located at the foot of a hill known as a Juju hill, which was supposed to be inhabited by spirits. We never climbed it. Juju is akin to a fetish or something that has magical powers. Our house was also just across from the tennis courts, so it was convenient and also handy for the players who could call in after raising a thirst on the court.

The local African tribe was called the Pagans to distinguish them from the predominant Hauser and Fulani. One day we saw a file of Pagans crossing our compound armed with spears. They were going to attack a neighboring clan. It was a fairly common occurrence for them, and as they were friendly to us it was an interesting sight. In fact, they used to bring us potatoes and other vegetables for sale. Megan was a bit embarrassed when she first began buying from them, since they wore the minimum of clothes, and sometimes nothing at all, and sat on their haunches. Usually the men did wear a sort of cap over the end of their penises.

Stanhope White, in his *Memoirs of a Nigerian Officer,* has this to say about the Pagans of the hills of Northern Nigeria: "The young men now met less desirable aspects of civilization. In the past a woman had to be a virgin until she was married, and that only after the payment of a very substantial bride price. Now instead of labouring for several years to obtain the bride price the youths found that in the Sodom of the plains temporary wives could be found for as long as their money lasted. Civilization had finally caught up with the hillman."

The Hausa were Muslims from the North. They wore flowing robes and turbans. They also did some trading, but our little shopping was mainly done in Jos. Even there only two or three small provision stores existed.

I was now faced with a staff problem. One of the married laboratory assistants came to my office and said that a stock inspector was paying unwelcome attention to his wife, and if this man appeared on his veranda again he would shoot him. He was serious, and I sent off an urgent telegram to the chief veterinary officer in Zaria asking that the stock inspector be transferred upcountry. I hinted at the reason. Action was immediately forthcoming much to my relief. Many of the stock inspectors were of the adventurous type—some had drifted up from South Africa and some were remittance men—and there was never a dull moment.

Vom was an isolated area and our white community was very small, numbering seven or eight at the most; but we never seemed at loss for something to do. Every morning at dawn I would ride one of the horses around the laboratory paddocks to check the stock and fences. In the evening we often timed our race horses down dirt tracks or played tennis. One of the staff had a piano so we enjoyed musical evenings. For Megan and I music has always played an important part in our lives. Someone had a radio but it was not easy to get the news from England in those days. It was too far away.

Nigeria was granted independence in 1960. A lot of effort went into the creation of a federation, but the hopes of the founders were not soon realized. There followed six years of corrupt politics and, in 1966, two military coups. In 1967 the Ibo rebelled and a tragic civil war raged for two and a half years. Democratic government has just recently been restored. The country is, however, comparatively peaceful. Economically, the country has a great future and this has been greatly enhanced by the discovery of oil. By 1963, Nigeria was the world's sixth largest oil producer.

But let's get back to Vom. Baby Joan contracted malaria. I took, stained, and examined the slide myself. The doctor came over from the leper colony and gave Joan an intramuscular injection. He sterilized the needle over a match flame, but Joan survived and for the time being the malaria abated.

It was soon time to proceed on leave, and we left Lagos on a German ship, the *Wangoni*. Joan came down with malaria again and the ship's doctor was treating her for seasickness. Fortunately, at Accra in the Gold Coast, a Scotch doctor from one of the mines came on board. He examined the patient and said that she had malaria—"You must fill her with liquids to avoid the complication of blackwater." So the original treatment was reversed. It worked, and as far as we know there has not been a recurrence of the disease in Joan.

We were anchored off Takoradi one evening and there were many large rowing boats alongside; this was the custom, as the

boats were filled with "boys" selling their African wares. For
some reason the captain ordered full steam ahead. I was on
deck at the time leaning over the side. The boats were in great
danger and many of them capsized. The men were thrown into
the water, and I thought many of them would be killed by the
big ship; but they were very strong swimmers and they all seemed
to survive. However, there was an undercurrent of antagonistic
feeling among the passengers, and the following day the captain
issued an apology.

4

CYPRUS

After my experience at the Vom laboratory, I wanted to continue my work on anaerobic diseases, and it was arranged that I should go to Cambridge University.

I applied for an appointment in a healthier climate and also was on the "short list" for an appointment in a research laboratory in Edinburgh, and I went there for an interview. What chance did I have when the other two candidates had surnames beginning with "Mac!" However, I enjoyed the trip to Scotland. I had been there before when I was stationed on Inchmickory, a very small island in the Firth, with the Royal Marines in 1918, and was to be there again as a delegate from Auburn University to the World International Poultry Congress in 1954. In Cambridge our son was born at the Milton Road Nursing Home. The obstetrician was a Cambridge Blue who later ran away with a nurse.

Soon after leaving Cambridge, I was appointed veterinary research officer in Cyprus. One of the main veterinary problems there was anthrax and the making of anthrax vaccine. There were few places where the techniques could be seen. The Colonial Office asked the Pasteur Institute in Paris if they would permit me to spend some time at the laboratory. This was refused. I think that at the time Pasteur's descendants had some restrictions on the manufacture of the vaccine. This was a disappointment but there was nothing we could do about it. So in 1930, with daughter Joan and new son Bill, we left for Cyprus.

We crossed the channel to Calais and went by train to Marseilles. Recently, we crossed the channel several times on the Hovercraft. There we took a Peninsular and Oriental ship to Port

Said. From there we caught a small packet for the overnight trip to the Southern Cypriot port of Larnaca, where we were met by Robin Roe, the chief veterinary officer. Robin was from Tipperary and, of course, was a good horseman. Our stock inspectors had been trained in Greece or Turkey. None were at that time fully qualified professionally. My laboratory assistant was a young Turk, recently out of secondary school. His name was Orhan, and he was a bright boy and was later to become chief veterinary officer.

I was soon at work in the veterinary laboratory, which was situated, with the chief veterinary officer's office, in the Municipal Gardens. Since I had been unable to visit the Pasteur Institute, I now contacted the South African laboratories in Ondersterpoorte. Doctors there had developed their own anthrax vaccine, using different strains of the organism depending on the species for which it was to be used. The goat was the most susceptible species. Our vaccine was successfully prepared and an annual vaccination campaign was commenced. It was, however, many years before the disease was eradicated. It had probably existed on the island for hundreds of years. No antibiotics were available then and there was no specific treatment, so one had to be careful in the handling of laboratory material. One of the men working there had a badly infected finger but survived. One day a military policeman came into the laboratory with half the carcass of a goat. I made and stained a microscopic smear and found it teeming with anthrax. I asked, "Where is the rest of the carcass?" The policeman said, "The villagers have eaten it." I phoned the hospital and was told that there was nothing much that we could do. Nothing happened. I theorized that infection would not occur if the mucous membrane was not broken. One day Robin Roe, the chief veterinary officer, brought to the laboratory a sample of sputum for examination. He said, "It is from my servant; give it a careful examination." Later he said, "How was the sputum?" I answered, "It was negative." He said, "That's great, it was *mine.*" He had a history of tubercular infection as a child.

Cyprus was free from rabies and strict quarantine regulations were in force. One of the problems was keeping tabs on wealthy yacht owners putting in and anxious to exercise their dogs. Pox was prevalent in sheep and goats. These were the early days in virus work, long before we had any idea that viruses had much to do in the way of morphology, and long before the day of the electron microscope. Our vaccine was made from desiccated scabs that were suspended in glycerosaline.

Our director of agriculture was Dawe, who had been director in Sierra Leone. Later, when he became director in what was then Palestine, he invited me to join his staff. Unfortunately, I had by then decided to return to England. Among our close friends were the Pitcairns. Andrew Pitcairn had been an agricultural officer in Tanganyika and when he retired he returned there and took up coffee farming. Our chief inspector was Antonis Petris, who some years later was accidentally shot and killed. His son studied in England and became chief veterinary officer, succeeding Orhan.

Our social life was pleasant. Cyprus is noted for its climate and scenery. Almost every weekend was spent at Kyrenia on the North Coast. Kyrenia is now in the Turkish zone. A favorite spot was Snake Island a few miles up the coast. Rarely would there be more than a dozen people about. Nearer to town was the castle where there was a natural sea pool. During the summer the women spent most of the time on Mount Troodos. As this is 6,000 feet high the climate is temperate while down in Nicosia it is very hot. The road was a gravel one and several of the bends had to be negotiated at two tries. We men used to go up on weekends, and after one quick trip down the mountain I became quite ill and was rushed to hospital, where I remained for a week. One night a chap with D.T.s was put into the ward. I left the next morning!

We acquired a piano and so our musical evenings were a joy. Such entertainment was better, I think, than the radio and T.V. that were to come. One night we put on a concert, at which artists sang in Greek, Turkish, English, Welsh, Irish, and Italian.

Frequent visitors were Weston, an agriculturist from Reading University, and Natrass, a mycologist whom we met many years later in Nairobi where he was with the East African Research Laboratory. In Cyprus Natrass was a confirmed bachelor and a very good tango dancer, which was popular then. I was no doubt a bit jealous. However he did get married and had two sons, both of whom were born in Kenya. The boys eventually had to face the possibility of leaving the country, a rather sad prospect for white people born in East Africa.

We had a donkey named Taffy who was a friend of the family and used to climb up the steps of the back porch and into the dining room. And I was able to enjoy horse riding again. One day Megan was going out riding and I thought her horse was a bit too fresh, so I decided to take him for a gallop to take some of the steam out of him. He soon threw me clear and in a complete somersault into a thorn bush! Nicosia had a popular race meeting. Most of the riders were professionals. I used to train horses owned by the Greeks, and they supplied the fodder. Most of the horses were thoroughbreds or of an Arab cross. It was exciting but I never had many winners. Equine sports were indeed popular, but when we introduced polo, we were short of players.

Cyprus has been influenced by Greek culture, and recently *Enosis,* or union with Greece, became a popular cry with the politically minded Greeks. It was, of course, opposed by the Turks. In the past political control had been exercised by Phoenicians, Greeks, Assyrians, Macedonians, Egyptians, Persians, Romans, Byzantines, Saracens, Franks, Venetians, Genoese, Turks, and the British. Greek Cypriots had long pressed for union with Greece. Turkey contended that if Britain gave up control of the island, it must be partitioned between Greek and Turkish Cypriots.

Ledra was the earliest name of Nicosia, the present capitol of Cyprus. In 280 B.C., when the town was *already* old, its name was changed to Leocosia, as it is still known by many Greeks. The name Cyprus is believed to be from the Greek *cuprus,* 'copper ore,' which has been mined there since Phoenician and Roman times. Now there is an American copper mine at Amiandes. Hellenic and Roman influences were evidently existent in A.D. 250.

In 1191 Richard the Lion Hearted, while on his way to the Holy Land, stopped to seize Cyprus and celebrated the victory by marrying Berengaria of Navarre in the town of Amanthus. Here she was crowned Queen of England. In the next year Richard transferred the island to Guy de Lusignan, who had been the Crusader king of Jerusalem. This dynasty held it for 300 years. Then came the Genoese and the Venetians to be followed by the Turks.

In 1931 riots broke out and other difficulties arose, which led to the suspension of the Legislative Council. As a government official, I was somewhat involved and so were the family. Our house was on the Troodos road about a mile out of Nicosia. One night when serious rioting broke out we were sitting at home and heard a mob approaching nearby. The two servants, one Greek and one Turkish, were in. I held my revolver on my knee. In the distance from a back window we could see Government House. Soon the sky was alight and we realized that the house was burning.

There was no sleep that night but we remained unharmed. In the morning we visited the Government House grounds and saw that the house had been completely destroyed. The governor, Sir Ronald Storrs, had apparently escaped through the back door. Sir Ronald, a friend of Lawrence of Arabia, had been governor of Jerusalem after the occupation by General Allenby, the first of his kind since Pontius Pilate. Allenby had defeated the Turks and this was the first appearance of Christians in the Holy Land since the Crusaders.

Rioting continued with us for many weeks. The British officials and their families were housed for the most part in one or the other of the two main hotels. During the next few weeks a number of government buildings were burned down, including the laboratory. We made over some of the horse boxes, and in spite of many difficulties, including the severe cold, we managed to continue the production of anthrax vaccine. Some British troops were flown in from Egypt. This was possibly the first time troops had been flown on active duty. It so happened that

I was sent by the commanding officer to the airfield with a message of greeting. I suppose in a way it was a rather historic occasion. Few realized perhaps at the time how the airplane would be used for military purposes in the future.

Megan and the children were with me and the pilot let them get into the cabin of the plane. Soon after this a dramatic incident occurred in which I was involved. Reports were received in Nicosia that disturbances were occurring in Kyrenia, where the bishop was in residence in his palace. A crowd had collected around the district commissioner's office, eventually damaging the building and pulling down the flag. A mob had moved to the grounds of the palace and some were threatening to attack certain buildings in the town, including a school and the hospital. I was ordered to Kyrenia with my Tudor Ford loaded to the footboards with soldiers and their gear. The crowd around the palace looked very dangerous and the sergeant deployed the men so as to prevent the mob from getting to the center of the town. However, there was a lot of rock throwing and the sergeant was hit on the jaw. A few shots were fired but no one was seriously injured. As night approached the mob became very ugly, and we tried to get a message to Nicosia for help. We found that the phone and telegraph wires had been cut, but eventually a messenger got through on a motorbike. About midnight help arrived in the form of a platoon of soldiers. Apparently the officer had received orders to arrest the bishop. He made a dramatic gesture by marching up to the door of the palace and shouting, "Open in the name of the king!" The door opened and standing in the hall at the foot of the winding staircase was the bishop and his retainers. A small party moved in, took hold of the bishop, and escorted him to a waiting truck. Meanwhile a young man in civilian clothes appeared, seemingly from no-where, and snipped off a small piece of the bishop's beard. This was an unfortunate and silly act and led to an inquiry later. At the time of the inquiry I was unable to appear, having been sent to the far end of the island. The bishop was deported. The now Archbishop Makarios of Nicosia, who also had been deported, and more recently fled the country, still heads the church of Cyprus, whose apostolic origin and autonomy were recognized by the Council of Ephesus in A.D. 431.

Makarios was deported with the bishop of Kyrenia in 1956. In his report on the deportation and referring to Makarios, governor Harding said, in part, "He remained silent while policemen and soldiers have been murdered, while women and children have been killed and maimed by bombs and even while he stood by the coffin of an Abbot of his own church who had been killed by terrorists in his own monastery. His silence has been accepted as approving these acts of violence." There is much more of this. In 1974 Makarios himself fled the country, under the protection of the British during a short-lived coup apparently engineered by a Greek officer clique and others. This led to the invasion by the Turks, after which Makarios returned again. It appeared that the Turks were now in a much better bargaining position.

After the riots in 1932 things became quiet politically. The Royal Welch Fusiliers left and were replaced by a company of the West Yorks. The damage to the veterinary buildings was repaired, and we resumed our normal work in the laboratory.

Our social activities resumed and so did horse riding and racing. In May we spent a few days in Famagusta. Then there was only one small hotel, and Famagusta was a very pleasant place. The tourist traffic in those days, although it existed, was not too noticeable. There were, and still are I presume, the ruins of 365 churches in the area, one for each day of the year—and of course there are the Roman ruins of Salamis.

We were now due for home leave and left Nicosia on June 30. We had an interesting trip, stopping at Athens, then going through the Corinth Canal to Brindisi and Trieste. We stopped one night in Milan and another in Basel, then a few days in London, during which time I called on the Veterinary College and research institutes. Some time was also spent at Liverpool University and the School of Tropical Medicine.

On our return to Cyprus we went via Calais, Paris, and Trieste. Here we boarded a Lloyd Triestino ship. After a few hours stop in Brindisi, we headed for the Corinth Canal. There was a delay at the entrance of the canal while some ships of

Mussolini's navy passed through. All our ship's officers were wearing Fascist badges and seemed a bit conscious of their new found aggressiveness.

After arriving in Nicosia we lived several weeks in the old Palace Hotel. Here we met the Queen Mother of Syria who was in exile.

We then moved into a house close to where the new government house was being built. One day Megan was playing with the children near the new building where she hurt her head. We called the doctor and for some reason he thought that a tetanus inoculation was necessary. The serum was made from horse serum, and, as it proved, Megan was allergic to the stuff. That evening we were changing to go out to dinner when she began to feel ill. She quickly developed a typical reaction with large subcutaneous swellings appearing over her body. I carried her to bed. There was nothing we could do except keep her absolutely still until the symptoms subsided. This we did and thankfully everything was much better in forty-eight hours.

Dawe, the director, now left to take up his new job as director in Palestine. This was in 1933 and it is interesting to note that the basis of an export industry in Jaffa oranges was then being laid down. Most of the farmers then were Arabs. Today citrus fruit is by far the largest commodity exported from Israel. In 1934 at the laboratory, the production of anthrax vaccine was going well and so was the annual vaccination program. There was one unpleasant incident when it was reported from one area that abcess formation was occurring in sheep following inoculation of vaccine. I isolated a staphylococcus from the site and submitted it to tests by exposing it to the same solution of glycerine saline as that in which the vaccine was suspended. It did not survive and we concluded that the infection was due to external contamination. Anyhow, we had no further trouble.

The results of some of the work in the Cyprus laboratory were later submitted to the University of Liverpool in the form of a thesis, and I was awarded the degree of M.V.Sc. Lord Derby was then the chancellor and he congratulated me as being the first to take the degree in Veterinary Science.

We returned to England at the end of the year. The local authorities were expanding their veterinary services, mainly because it had been decided to tackle the problem of tuberculosis in cattle. Dawe had invited me to join him in Palestine, and I was sorely tempted but we finally decided to leave the Colonial Service. Also our two children were now of school age. I was soon appointed veterinary officer in Stafford. I missed the laboratory very much and at the back of my mind was the thought that one day I would return. I was appointed the first veterinary officer at the city of Stoke on Trent. Stoke had visions of being the first city to have a regional abattoir, of which there were to be four in the whole country.

This scheme did not go through and it still has not been developed. Upon my appointment the Ministry of Agriculture expanded the staff. This meant the elimination of many local veterinary officers and others. The conditions offered by the ministry to the local officials were quite bad, and the opportunity to present one's case was denied, so that the plight of many, including myself, was so unsatisfactory that the possibility of striking was actually seriously considered. We finally had to agree to the ministry's terms of nationalization. I was taken on and held at the same salary scale until the end of the war, when I resigned the service and left the country.

5

THE UNITED KINGDOM

During the two years since leaving Cyprus, we had lived in Stoke, Barlaston, and Keele. I became a fan of the Stoke City soccer team. This was the time when Stanley Matthews, perhaps the finest player of all time, was rising to stardom. Another star was Frankie Soo, who was surely a rarity, being the only Chinese player in England.

One cannot leave the Potteries without making mention of the fact that this is one of the most famous centers for the manufacturing of chinaware in the world. The names of Spode, Minton, and Copeland are familiar. The Wedgwood Company had recently moved out of the center of the city to Barlaston, where they constructed a modern factory that eliminated most of the air pollution. Josiah Wedgwood, 1730-1795, was the founder of the company. He was a potter and chemist, and his father had been a potter too. Josiah's daughter was the mother of Charles Darwin. The Wedgwood family had lived in the village for many years, and one day we had the pleasure of going to the house for tea with Mrs. Wedgwood.

The Ministry of Agriculture now stationed me in Bangor— a cathedral and college city off the coast of North Wales. The following year we were on the way to Le Touquet but we got no further than London. The war had started; I lost my hotel deposit.

Since our trip to Le Touquet was now impossible, we headed north after a brief stay with my parents in London. One of the very first little events of the war was, of course, the blackout, which meant that no lights could be visible after sunset. All houses and office windows had to be fitted with curtains through which no light could pass. All car lamps were fitted with covers

51

so that only a bare crack of light was visible. This we had to do before we left London. We were going to stay the night with the Linfords in Tamworth. We arrived in a town after dark. I found a policeman and said, "I am looking for Tamworth." He answered, "You are there." The next day we headed for Blackpool on the Lancashire coast. We managed to find a hotel. This was full of pregnant women who had been evacuated from Liverpool. The blackout was now fairly complete and at night we were allowed only candles. The evacuation of women and children from the cities to the countryside or to areas considered comparatively safe was successfully carried out, although it created some problems.

We returned to Bangor and the following spring the air raids on Liverpool began. We were on the flight route and sometimes German bombs fell on Bangor. One dark night two German airmen bailed out in the nearby hills. I was in the Home Guard and went out with the search party. One was found dead in his parachute. The other was taken alive, brought down the mountain, and, in a cafe owned by a friend of mine, revived with a cup of tea! In the Home Guard we initially trained with broom handles. We dug trenches at strategic points and every night played our part in the watch over the skies. I was in our barracks when the first rifles arrived from Canada. This was a red letter day.

Everything including petrol and foodstuffs was now rationed. We were lucky in that Megan's parents were farming in Felin y Coed, a beautiful little village near Llanrwst. From time to time we were able to have fresh eggs and homemade butter. The Welsh letter F is sounded like the English V, and this gives the word Felin y Coed a soft sound well suited to its meaning, the "Mill in the Wood," and also to its background of green trees and hills. It does, I think, typify the beautiful countryside so commonplace in North Wales.

We lived in a bungalow overlooking the Menai Bridge, which extends from the Bangor side over the straits to the island of Anglesea. At one time it was thought that the Germans might invade by way of Ireland and so perhaps into Wales. In any case, trenches were dug adjacent to our bungalow and sometimes were manned by regular troops. Véry lights were often fired off much to the delight of Joan and Bill and their school friends.

Megan, with her musical associations in the area, was able to take part in some concerts and this brought relaxation to the troops stationed in the vicinity. She thought that Joan had a good voice, and we were lucky in that Rosina Buckman, a famous opera star from New Zealand who was teaching at the Royal Academy of Music in London, had a cottage in Anglesea where she and her husband, Maurice D'Oisley, visited from time to time. Rosina had been on a world tour with the great Melba. Maurice was also a fine professional pianist. We came to know them well and often met in London after we moved to the south of England. In 1941 Rosina came to our house to hear Joan sing. She seemed very pleased and said, "I must have her in London for training." In a few months Joan was awarded a John Thomas Scholarship at the Royal Academy. A qualification of the scholarship was that at least one of the candidate's parents had to be Welsh. At this time Joan was attending Saint Winifred's Girls School in Lanfairfechan. Bill was at Hillgrove Preparatory School and doing well, so well in fact that we hoped to get him into one of the better English public schools. This was a reversal from my own experience, since I had attended an American public school, which was more comparable to an English day school. We are still discussing the pros and cons of the two methods. Bill stresses the merit of the American system with the mixing of the sexes and freer choice of subjects, while I stress the advantages of the English public school system. Academically, the British method certainly puts the pupil at least one year ahead of his American counterpart with a good grounding in the Classics. I happen to think that this is important but many people would, I am sure, disagree. The question of character building is, of course, of great importance, particularly in this rapidly changing world. A discussion of the importance of education in this area and the relative merits of different systems is too wide a subject to be dealt with here.

I had been studying the entrance requirements for a number

of public schools, and, in fact, when possible we visited some of them. Epsom College, which was considered one of the best schools, offered a Densham Scholarship. This was for the sons of parents who had given meritorious service to the empire. I had the temerity to inquire about it, and Bill was requested to sit for the examination. He did very well and was awarded the scholarship. This meant that his tuition and board at this fine school would be taken care of. We were very pleased not only because of Bill's good exam results but because like many others at that time, financial problems were aggravated by wartime conditions. So in spite of the air raids on London, which were being intensified, Bill went off to Epsom at the tender age of twelve.

One evening I was called to a case at a small farm situated at the foot of Snowden. At 3,500 feet it is the highest mountain in Wales—not high by most standards but rugged and beautiful. The country around has a weird and eerie appearance. This night the sky was stormy and dark with lowering thunderclouds hanging around the mountain. I could not get all the way to the farm in the car, a Model-T Ford, so I had to walk across the last few fields. I knocked at the farmhouse door and was let into the large kitchen. Sitting in front of a blazing fire was a beautiful young girl with a delicate rose-tinted complexion, flowing red hair, and large luminous eyes. It was a striking picture but the poor girl was mentally deranged. I was shocked. The strange atmospheric conditions outside and the weird scene inside the house affected me considerably, and I never forgot the incident.

Veterinary work for the Ministry of Agriculture in Wales was largely concerned with the tuberculin testing of cattle. Wales, like parts of Scotland, was a comparatively clean area of Britain. It was work of a routine nature and did not require much initiative. There was some element of excitement when testing young stock in that the Welsh cattle carried long horns and were big and wild. At least once a year sheep were gathered from the mountainside to be dipped. This was aimed at the eradication of sheep scab, a parasitic skin disease that causes serious damage to the wool. This meant of course a delightful chance of seeing the shepherd and his Welsh sheepdog at work with such wonderful artistry, collecting and separating the flocks. It was only after many years of persistent work that the disease was eradicated from Britain.

There were also occasional concentrations of staff during outbreaks of foot and mouth disease. The slaughter policy was in force. All cattle, sheep, and pigs that were infected or in close contact with the disease were slaughtered and the farmers were compensated. Strangely enough, in much of the Americas the disease is called hoof and mouth, even in scientific circles, although it really does not attack the hoof but rather the underlying tissues. A severe outbreak now occurred in the very densely cattle populated area of the county of Cheshire. Veterinary staff were concentrated there for several weeks. This was at the time of Hitler's air raids on the ports of Britain. Liverpool was one port city that was on the verge of collapse when the raids stopped. Strangely, the Luftwaffe attacks on the cathedral cities and even the moonlight raids ceased as well. They seemed to come to an end just at the critical time. One night after a heavy raid on Liverpool, Dr. Brooks, one of my colleagues on the foot and mouth team, and I decided to go into town to see the opera at the old Royal Court Theater. As we were going in, teams of worn-out firemen were returning to their headquarters in the suburbs. The show went on but the port had received a very severe battering during the previous twenty-four hours. One weekend, Megan and the two children, and also the three chow pups, came up to Chester from Bangor for a few days. They were in a hotel one night, but they had to leave because of a lack of accommodation. The night after they moved out the hotel was bombed out. We had a number of very narrow escapes during the war but thankfully we were protected. In Chester two of the Chow pups were bought by the army. They preferred them to Alsatians as guard dogs.

One day I went on to a farm on which foot and mouth disease had been confirmed just after the farmer had let three heifers out of a shed in which they had been confined for some time. As soon as they saw daylight they took off across country.

Here was a problem with three animals from an infected farm
running amok in a very heavily stocked area. There was nothing
to do but call on the army for help. This was soon available,
but it was some time before the poor animals could be maneuvered
into a position so that they could be shot without endangering
the public. It was a miracle that no infection was spread, but it
was a difficult report to write!

Hitler now ordered the fire raids to begin, and in the mornings the fields in many of the farms would be covered with spent
bomb cases; but few fires were caused outside the big cities. In
his autobiography Quentin Reynolds says:

> One of the most fearful experiences we had in London was
> the blitz which destroyed much of the city by fire. At the
> height of the fire raids I went to the roof of the Savoy Hotel
> to see the extent of the fire. Across the Thames there was a
> mile of solid flame. The greedy fingers of the flames stretched
> high into the night and we felt sure they would reach the
> Houses of Parliament on our side of the river. Looking
> down the Strand we could see the Dome of Saint Paul's
> lighted by the fires of hundreds of burning buildings. None
> of what I was watching seemed real to me. Sometimes you
> can believe fiction when your mind rejects reality.

Soon after the fire raids I was transferred to Hampshire in
the south of England. We stored our furniture at first in Pick-
fords in London. One day I received a telegram from them.
It read: "Regret your furniture completely destroyed by enemy
action." A few days later we went up to London and found that
we could salvage quite a number of things including the Turkish
rug Orhan had given us in Cyprus, although it was damaged
by fire. We still have the rug, which is an interesting memento
of the air raids on London.

Bill was still in school at nearby Epsom College, and Joan
was at the Royal Academy of Music. On one of the few times
that Joan missed her morning train to London, it was bombed
as it arrived in Waterloo station and a number of passengers

were killed. However, we were all often in London and Bill would come and join us for the day when he could get out of school. Like all schools, Epsom had its air raid shelters in the school grounds. Being so near London they saw much aerial activity, including some of the Battle of Britain. Bombs were dropped in and near the school grounds. I was now out of the Home Guard but like many other civilians, I stood fire watch at the office several nights a week. We were entertaining the military almost every night during the week. It kept Megan busy but I think she enjoyed it. We had a piano and so had many musical evenings. No need for radio or television. We all benefited. The boys enjoyed a taste of home life, and we enjoyed their company and of course benefited by sharing their rations. Air raids were a daily and nightly occurrence. The wail of the siren was commonplace.

One day at Winchester school grounds I met a Capt. Arthur Wood, an artillery officer in the American army. He was watching the boys play cricket, rather an unlikely occupation for a native of Oklahoma. However, he came up for supper several times, and one day at the YMCA he met his brother, David, who was a fighter pilot. They had not met since joining up and this called for a party at our house. Later, whenever David went on a mission he used to dip his wings when he flew over our house. Another frequent visitor was Pvt. Dick Thatcher. At first we thought he was a bit slow sharing his rations, but one day he staggered in with a full duffel bag of rations, which he had been hoarding up. After the war he remained in Europe and studied law at the Sorbonne, later to practice in Washington and Los Angeles.

News now came through that many of the women and children whom we knew in Cyprus had been sent to South Africa. Our particular friend, Andrew Pitcairn, who was agricultural officer in Cyprus, had gone into the army and had been taken prisoner in Crete. He was in the Lubec prisoner-of-war camp for many months. As soon as he was released he was returned to England and immediately visited us. We were struck by the strange effect that being a prisoner of war had had on

Andrew's personality. He seemed to be lost and completely out of touch with what was going on in the world. He was soon able to get out to South Africa to join his family. Eventually they made their way to Tanzania and went coffee farming at Mbosi Mbeya in the Highlands. They were happy there but the farm was not, I think, a great financial success. We met often over the years, usually at the Commonwealth Club in London. With the coming of independence to Tanzania things became difficult and Andrew and the family returned to England, but his heart remained in East Africa.

One weekend we went up to Desford School near Leicester where my brother-in-law was teaching. One night we had to get into the air raid shelter in the school yard. It was the night of the big raid on Coventry when much of the center of the city, including the cathedral, was destroyed. At our safe distance it was a dramatic sight. Many years later we visited the city. This was after the ultra-modern cathedral had been built. The ruins of the old church still stand adjacent and make a dramatic contrast.

As I was now in charge of the Southampton area, we had to find a house there. The one we found was something of a miracle, since housing was almost impossible to find. The place had been a large coach house belonging to an estate, converted for use as army offices and then abandoned. It was a nice location on the Basset Avenue exit from Southampton to Winchester. From the front gate one could see the funnels of the *Queen Mary* when she was in dock.

There our meetings with the military stepped up. The southern part of England was now literally an armed camp. In 1944, R.A.F. and American raids on the continent were almost continuous day and night. "D-Day" was fast approaching and on that great day I was down the coast and had a wonderful view of the action above and on the Channel. Megan was at home in Southampton, which was very much in the front line. I returned home in the evening and for several days was busy on the docks. Many of the wounded and the prisoners were arriving. Some of them brought back dogs, and because of the danger of the introduction of rabies into the country, these animals had to be found and put into quarantine. One case created considerable interest in the London newspapers. In a room on the docks I found a large Saint Bernard dog tied to the arms of a sleeping sailor. Eventually the dog was taken over by a Wren who paid the quarantine expenses. Another doggie story at the end of the war concerned a pup that had been smuggled into England and later onto the *Queen Mary*. This was against the law of course. However, the G.I. wrote to Joan, "Tell your Dad we had the dog in the duffel bag."

The V-1 and V-2 rockets were directed at London. Londoners were becoming very tired. Five years of war with all its problems and tragedies were enough. The horrible thing about the V-2 was that it arrived and exploded without warning. It was nerve-racking and bad for the morale. Thankfully, the rocket bases in the Netherlands were soon captured. For those in Britain this was the beginning of the war's end.

About this time we had an outbreak of foot and mouth disease, which started on a pig farm near the coast. It had apparently been caused by infection from foodstuffs imported from the Argentine, where the disease was then endemic. The wartime blackout was still on and we were not allowed to burn the carcasses, which had to be buried instead. The land was very swampy and the work difficult. The next day I visited the burial site and found the feet of many of the animals above the surface of the ground; the last thing we wanted to see. The problem was solved by calling out the Royal Navy with its powerful pumps. We were able to drain off most of the water and have the offending parts covered.

When Bill was home from Epsom we sometimes went to see Southampton play soccer. Twenty years later, when on one of our many visits to London, we went to see them play a local team, the Queens Park Rangers. This time my grandson John, aged nine, was with us.

On V-E Day Megan and I went up to London. All schoolchildren had the day off. Bill came up from Epsom and Joan met us. So we were together on that historic occasion with millions of others who flocked to the city that had suffered a great deal during the war. The streets were jammed with people and there was music, dancing, and rejoicing. We had been warned to take some sandwiches with us. This we did and ate them sitting on the back of one of the famous lions in Trafalgar Square. During the afternoon Sir Winston Churchill came out onto the balcony of one of the government buildings in Whitehall to address the people. We managed to get down Whitehall to see and hear it all. What a memorable moment! We are constantly reminded of it on our frequent visits to London since the Commonwealth Society, of which we are members, is situated in Trafalgar Square.

With the end of the war on Europe, it was time for American military personnel to return home. Many of them returned on the *Queen Mary*. A friend of ours, Colonel Scherf, was in charge of the shipping of the troops and was often at our house on Basset Avenue. Now the people of Jersey, which had been occupied by the Germans, commenced once again to send their famous Jersey cattle to England. I was in charge, of course, of the quarantine station at the docks. As a symbolic gesture of its gratitude the Jersey government presented a Jersey cow to Sir Winston. The *London Telegraph* sent a reporter down, and so with the famous cow I had my photo in the London press. At times we had quite a number of cattle in the quarantine. The government would not permit the sale of the milk, and so it was given away. There was often plenty of cream in our house, a treat after years of wartime austerity. Colonel Scherf would bring blocks of ice off the *Queen Mary* and ice-cream powder from who knows where, and with some assistance from other military friends we would set to making lovely ice-cream.

We had many enjoyable evenings at the house on Basset Avenue, which was called Yew Tree Cottage, meeting people from all over the world. One night we entertained people from twelve different countries. One of them was our old friend Norman Hall, on leave from Sierra Leonne. Little did we think that seven years later he would follow me to an assignment in Iraq for the United Nations.

6

THE UNITED STATES

After a rather frustrating professional experience in the Ministry of Agriculture, culminating in the incident when they did not inform me of the request of Governor Blood for my services for duty in the laboratory in West Africa, I was anxious to get away. I wrote to my cousin, Jeff Holt, who was a veterinarian in practice on Long Island, New York. We used to visit Jeff at Huntington when we lived on Staten Island. He suggested that I should go over there to look things over. Uncle Bill would sponsor me. I applied for leave and sailed for New York on the S.S. *United States*. We were four days late in arriving. The captain said it was the worst trip he had ever made, and we made the headlines in the New York papers. I spent most of the trip in my bunk. On going ashore my first impressions were the bright lights, the abundance of food in the shops, and the way people were wasting paper, string, and other such items that we had been lacking for so many years.

I did not want to go into practice so before leaving England I had arranged a number of interviews in the States. I had two meetings with Colonel Kelser, a well-known microbiologist and dean of the Veterinary School at the University of Pennsylvania. His idea was for me to take charge of a new equine research station. However, the necessary funds did not materialize. Another meeting was with Dean Sugg at the Veterinary School of the University of Auburn, Alabama. My train arrived in Auburn from New York at midnight. Having left New York in the early morning, I was ready for bed. I stepped down off the train to find the dean there to meet me. He said, "Let's go to the office and have a chat." We talked at some length into the early hours and the outcome was that I was offered and accepted

61

the position of Professor of Preventive Medicine, partly, I think, because of my experience in dealing with this subject in Uganda, Nigeria, and Cyprus.

I returned to New York and now in order to remain in the United States I had to obtain a permanent immigration visa. For some reason, which I still do not understand, in order to obtain this one has to go out of the country and then return. So like many others in similar circumstances I went up to Montreal. I found the long-distance trains in the States very comfortable and fast, but some of the local trains were not so good. The first night in Montreal I went into a movie house and came out into a howling blizzard. I suppose it was a fitting introduction to Canada. At the immigration office I was informed that I would need a police record from all the places in which I had lived during the last fifteen years. This meant about seven places in Britain and a similar number overseas. I went back to my hotel and phoned Megan to give her the news. The next morning these requirements seemed ridiculous and so I returned to the immigration office. This time I saw a senior official. I explained the seeming impossibility of the requirements and he said, "Get a note from the police in Southampton and one from the Colonial Office and that will be satisfactory." This sounded much more reasonable and so I phoned Megan again. I think that by now she was beginning to wonder what was going on!

I returned to Long Island for a few days. The sights and sounds of New York suburbs reminded me of my school days on Staten Island. I was soon on my way to Auburn to assume what proved to be a most interesting and rewarding assignment. I believe the salary then for a full professor was $5,000 per annum. I now met some of my new colleagues—Dr. Charles Roberts, just returned from the Pacific, and Dr. Crandell, just returned from England. The dean asked me to assist Dr. Roberts in the State Diagnostic Laboratory and at the same time to prepare to teach pathology. Later I taught poultry diseases. There was a staff shortage and the postwar rush of students was on. Housing was a problem but finally I obtained one of the army huts which were being used by faculty and students.

In the state laboratory we were confronted with Newcastle disease, which threatened the poultry industry—a primary concern in the country. This disease had apparently been quiescent in California for many years without having been diagnosed. Some years earlier Jimmy Doyle, a friend of mine at the Veterinary Research Laboratory of the Ministry of Agriculture, was investigating a serious outbreak of disease in Newcastle, England. He thought that perhaps it was fowl plague, a disease he had encountered previously in Egypt. He compared sera from the two diseases and found that they were different. Doyle examined some sera from California and found that it indeed was the same as that from the Newcastle disease. About then a similar condition occurred in the East Indies. In Auburn Dean Sugg suggested that I plot the outbreaks as they occurred. However, the disease spread so rapidly throughout the United States that this soon became superfluous. It became a national problem where poultry were intensively produced and led to a great deal of research and vaccine production.

Prior to the fall term I returned to England to bring over the family. I went tourist class on the *Queen Mary*. Most of the passengers were students. I had not been fit and Megan had two young doctors waiting for me. They could find nothing seriously wrong.

I am sure the children were not keen on leaving England. Later on they became reconciled to the idea and perhaps in some agreement. Looking back, one wonders what would have happened if the move had not been made. At the time I was happy about the move, since professionally I was in a rewarding position after a frustrating experience during the war. Moving a family from one country to another should broaden the experience of the individuals, and if the good things of the former culture are retained the end must be beneficial. Megan and I had already lived and worked in five different countries.

Megan had a buyer for the house. One piece of furniture that I still regret leaving was a sideboard of Belgian oak dated 1776. Getting passenger tickets across the Atlantic at that time was difficult. Bill went on the *Mauretania* and the rest of us on the

Queen Mary. This was to be almost our last trip by sea. It seemed that the era of the sea was about to be replaced by that of the air.

The classes in Auburn were large and I often had classes of 60 senior veterinary students. More than 90 percent of them were ex-service men, many of whom had served in England, so we established a good rapport. This helped the process of learning. They were keen students. There was one brilliant man who always sat in the front row near the lecture podium. He kept me very much on the alert. Of course, we had the odd one who in the warm Alabama summer enjoyed pushing off his shoes and having a nap.

On the staff was Professor Emeritus Cotton, who was associated with Dr. Buck in Washington in the discovery of Strain 19 vaccine, which has been used all over the world in the control of contagious abortion in cattle. This was a disease in which I became increasingly involved, leading finally to making a survey of its occurrence in the whole of Rhodesia for the government.

I believe the whole family enjoyed the life at the university. I found my greatest satisfaction in teaching, and there was the added bonus of diagnostic and research work at the State Diagnostic Laboratory.

Poultry diseases were of great importance in the South. It was in Georgia that the great "broiler" industry was born. These states are still able to produce and ship ready-to-be broiled chickens across the United States, a ninety-six hour trip, and undersell the California market. They had been quick to develop a completely integrated industry. Once I was asked to go over to Georgia to investigate an outbreak that was causing the deaths of thousands of young turkeys. The only organism that was constantly isolated was the genus Proteus, considered generally to be nonpathogenic. I did some research confirming reports in medical literature that under certain conditions the organism was an important pathogen.

I became faculty adviser to the foreign students, something which gave Megan and me great pleasure. Many of the students came from South America, but some came from India, Greece, Israel, Lebanon, Thailand, Pakistan, Iran, Jordan, Kenya, Puerto

Rico, Guatemala, and Holland. One outstanding meeting was
when a Jewish and an Arab student presented their views. The
Arab had lost his home in the 1948 war. Those interested in
the Middle East should study the history of that part of the world
over the last seventy years. It would help them understand the
position of the Palestinian Arab.

Campus life was never dull. Apart from teaching and research,
there was the pleasure of meeting visiting lecturers and musicians.
One visitor was Jennie Torel, the Metropolitan Opera star whom
I had met previously on the *Queen Mary*. Professor Beveridge,
from the Veterinary School at Cambridge University, paid us a
visit, as did Professor Polding from the East African school just
starting in Nairobi. Polding had previously worked in Malta, and
we had common ground in our mutual interest in brucellosis.
When this disease was found by Dr. Bruce in the military personnel on Malta in 1887, it was given the name of Malta fever. I
met Polding again in 1957 when we were in Nairobi prior to
returning to Israel after working in Ethiopia with the U.S. aid
program. At the time of his visit to Auburn, the Mau Mau
uprising was in full spate and he was sensitive to the fact that
he was moving around without his revolver; he was not too
impressed by our "chromium-plated civilization," as he called
it. What changes, for the better or worse, have taken place in
East Africa and the United States since then! Another veterinarian
who came was Pat Guilbride from Jamaica. He came to attend
some lectures at the rabies laboratory in Montgomery. Pat had
been born in Rhodesia, in which country I later worked.

Bill had settled down and worked toward a degree in Engineering Physics. Joan continued her vocal studies and eventually
received an audition at the Metropolitan Opera House in New
York. The maestro, Max Rudolph, informed me that she was a bit
young but that if she came back in six months time there was a
distinct possibility that she would be signed on. However, much
to our disappointment, Joan decided that she did not want to
continue her career in music. Later she married Gordon Howell,
an Auburn graduate who was an officer in the air force. Bill

graduated and obtained his master's in Physics. He immediately obtained an appointment with the Bell Telephone Labs in New York.

The U.S. Government had started a national campaign for the eradication of bovine brucellosis. This entailed the blood testing and removal of reacting cattle. With others, I did some work showing that the agglutination test was positive in milk from infected cows. However, a positive reaction was also obtained with all colostrum and milk from drying off cows. These were, of course, false positive reactions and had to be taken into account when testing milk.

In 1951 I attended the World Congress on brucellosis in Washington. There I met Dr. Kesteven, Head of the Animal Health Division of the Food and Agricultural Organization of the United Nations. Some months later he invited me to take an assignment as veterinary microbiologist to the Iraq government.

7

IRAQ

There was a friendly atmosphere in Auburn—perhaps part of the Southern tradition—and I was enjoying my teaching and the work in the State Diagnostic Laboratory. However the Baghdad assignment sounded very interesting and I accepted, having first received a leave of absence from Auburn. It was November when we started on our journey, and in Atlanta the weather was so bad that the planes were all grounded. We had to proceed by train. Bill with his usual consideration had booked seats for us at the Metropolitan. The next day we went on board our plane, a four-propeller Constellation, and looking back we saw Bill waving some insurance tickets!

We spent some time in England and Wales visiting our folks, and visited the laboratory of the Ministry of Agriculture. Then on to Rome—a city that we visited subsequently on many occasions and never ceased to enjoy. The Food and Agricultural Organization offices are in a building that Mussolini called the Africa building. From the roof there is a wonderful panoramic view of the city. I was in Rome ostensibly for briefing, but I was told that I was to be the guinea pig in Baghdad!

Early in January we left Rome for Baghdad via Cairo. I was anxious to see an Egyptian microbiologist there who had been a fellow student of mine at Liverpool, but Megan and I were not allowed out of the airport. Possibly our passports were not in order, but I was not even allowed to use the telephone. There was much political unrest in the city at that time, and the airport was very much a restricted area.

On the day we arrived in Baghdad, there had been a public hanging in the main street. This was rather an unusual sort of welcome. We were, however, immediately fascinated by the teeming life of the city with its donkeys and camels taking issue with cars in the streets. At that time the main street, Al Rachid, was riddled with potholes and a ride on a bus was like riding on a roller coaster. However, it was fascinating and the people were kind and friendly.

To get to the laboratory I relied on a government vehicle to pick me up each day. Fadil, a quiet and unassuming Iraqui, was my driver for the whole year. Private transportation was often a problem, but with the aid of kind friends and a fondness for walking we managed quite well. Looking back one wonders how Megan walked so often to the club in the evening with the temperature near the 100 mark. The pool and the pleasant company were the attractions. We gave little thought to any possible danger in the streets.

My first visit to the laboratory was something of a shock. There was a very strong smell from the open drain that ran by the front door, sufficient to make me feel a bit nauseated; but I got used to it. This kind of a drain, often called a jube and running down the middle of the street, was very common in the Middle East and still is in some places.

It was now about ten years since the termination of the British mandate, and apparently because of lack of funds or other reasons there had been a sad regression in many areas. There was very little equipment in the laboratory and there was no current scientific literature in the library. It was obvious that the "guinea pig" was going to have plenty to do.

In the beginning I had to go to the central medical hospital to borrow microscope slides and any other bits of equipment that I could get thanks to the kindness of the Scottish professor of Medicine, who was also interested in my favorite subject of brucellosis. At the medical department I also met the visiting professor from the university of Amsterdam—Dr. DeFrew.

So at work I started from scratch. There were two qualified veterinarians—Nadjmi Deen, a graduate of Cairo University, and Hassan. The former acted as my interpreter.

Iraq had changed little since the end of the WWI in 1918.

Before the turn of the century, British and German influence was evident. Internally the Iraqis had been unhappy with the Turkish regime. The German drive through Turkey and the British interest in Arabia eventually led to the creation of the nation of Iraq. The Turks were driven from the area by the British army in which there were Indian regiments. The Turks suffered nearly 100,000 casualties. The armistice of Mudros left the three Turkish provinces of Mosul, Baghdad, and Bashra under British control. The conception of the mandate under the League of Nations developed at this time. It was applied in a number of different ways to a number of areas including Iraq and Palestine. The British mandate extended from 1920 to 1932. Even at this time the Iraqi and Iranian oil fields were beginning to exercise their influence on international affairs, and the future of these countries became of great interest to the big oil companies.

Article 22 of the Covenant of the League of Nations said, in part, "To those Colonies and Territories which as a consequence of the late war have ceased to be under the sovereignty of the States which formerly governed them and which are inhabited by peoples not yet able to stand by themselves, there should be applied the principle that the well being and welfare of such peoples form a sacred trust of civilization, and securities for this trust should be the principle consideration in the selection of the Mandatory. . . ." Some difficult years followed though.

The British taxpayer became very tired of the word *Mesopotamia*. A second treaty of alliance with Iraq was signed in 1932, by which Britain retained the use of three air bases. During the early part of the Second World War, the Middle East was in a tenuous position. In 1941 the British landed troops in Basrah and the German threat to Iraq was thereafter much under control. Just over ten years after the end of the war the king of Iraq was killed, and there has been a military regime in power almost continuously ever since.

Shortly after our arrival in Iraq, we were invited to dinner at the home of Sir John Troutbeck, the British ambassador. Among the guests were Mr. Wooley, the first secretary whose brother was chief adviser to the Kawait government, and Haideri

Bey, the director of agriculture. I had the feeling that my political views were being assessed.

On the job I had some well-defined projects to work on to first properly equip the laboratory, to formulate plans for a new veterinary research center, to bring the library up to date, and to widen the scope of all the veterinary activities. In drawing up the plans we were fortunate in having the help of a young British architect who was working for the government. The chief veterinary officer for some reason would often file the plans away, but finally they were approved. It was, however, several years after I left before work commenced at Abu Ghraib some miles north of the city where there already was a college of agriculture. Equipment for the immediate use of the old laboratory was ordered and in about three months it began to arrive.

I soon became aware that the milk supply to the city was a serious problem. It came mainly from a herd of buffalo owned by the Honorable Hikmat Sulieman—a former prime minister. We found that the herd was heavily infected with brucellosis. We had the delicate task of breaking the news to the owner and to inform him that the reactors would have to be removed. This meant some delicate negotiations. Megan and I went to his house for tea. There we met his beautiful wife who spoke French and Arabic but no English. We did eventually have the herd tested, which confirmed a high incidence of brucella. These buffalo were wild and difficult to bleed, and we frequently resorted to the Milk Ring Test on which I had been doing research for a number of years. The hygenic conditions on the farm were very bad. I had consulted with the World Health Organization and with the help of their local representative a pasteurization plant was set up. This resulted in a great improvement in the milk supply to the city. During the time we lived there, Megan bought our milk from an Iraqi woman who brought her cow around to the front door and milked her on the spot.

Some animal deaths were occurring in various parts of the country and the farmers believed they were due to chemicals being used in the locust control campaign in which the Shell Company was involved. The affair caused quite a furor and the company sent a man out from New York to look into it. I was asked to make an investigation. This I did, carrying out feeding experiments and spraying areas of lucerne with lindane. Cattle, sheep, and goats were fed with no ill effects. I hoped that the chemical company would give some support for additional work, but this was not to be.

I was now given the opportunity to visit various veterinary centers in different parts of the country. This was very productive professionally and also gave me the chance to see parts of the country so historically linked with the cradle of Western civilization. Megan always came with me and so did Nadjmi Deen.

On one trip to the northern part of the country, we stopped one night at the hotel in Mosul. The temperature was 120 degrees and the air conditioner was not working. I found that the only way to keep fairly cool was to remain submerged in the bath during the afternoon. At night, with about forty Arab men, we slept communal style on the roof. It was an unusual experience— especially for Megan! It was a bright moonlight night and one could hear the jackals calling in the desert. While in Mosul we visited the ruins of Nineveh. Strangely enough there is little to see except acres of gently rolling hills of sand and some enormous sculptured bulls forming parts of ancient gateways. Standing on the site, however, one can still imagine the great expanse of the old city, and here one can be transported back to the dawn of civilization. Much of the art and statuary that was here can be found in the London and Berlin museums.

Nineveh was the third capital of Assyria after Assur and Nimrud. The son of Tiglath Peleser made it his capital about 1080 B.C. He built a temple to Ishta the Goddess of Love and War. Four hundred years later Sennecherib carried out vast building operations. Lugard the famous British explorer described the buildings as paneled with alabaster slabs and bas-reliefs with portals of colossal winged bulls. All the resources were drawn upon. The king introduced cotton from Egypt and brought clean water by canal from 50 miles away. Esarhaddon, son of Sennecherib, built more palaces. These ruins were preserved until the nineteenth century. One of the most remarkable treasures in the world, the king's libary of religious, scientific, and literary works, is also lodged in the British Museum. He had been educated in Babylon and translated Sumerian texts into Assyrian. To him we owe the *Epic of Gilgamesh,* the Babylonian version of the Deluge. Nineveh fell in 607 B.C. to the Medes.

We left Mosul very early one morning for Sursang—a beautiful Kurdish village in the mountains close to the Persian border. The altitude was 3,750 feet and it was cool. The Prince Regent had a farm here and we inspected the animals. At the hotel all the guests were Jews from Israel or Lebanon. The following day we walked over the nearby hill to a Christian village. It was a picturesque place. Here was a Nestorian church. The Nestorians separated from the ancient Eastern Church in the year 300 and spread eastward through Northern Iraq, Iran, India, and China. While walking through the village we saw a sick boy lying on a bed. He was suffering from small pox. We stayed another day in this interesting village and at the invitation of the priest went to a service in the Nestorian church; but first the father invited us to sit outside and drink some leben. The door to the church was low and we had to bow to get through it. We were told that perhaps the reason for the low door was that any Moslem getting into the church would have to bow to the cross. The church was very small and the floor was of dirt. A few chairs were brought in but most of the people stood up. There seemed to be no windows and the light came from flickering candles. There was a lot of incense burning and the hand of the priest was frequently kissed. The readings were in Aramaic, which had been the predominant language in the Middle East in biblical times.

We inspected the livestock on the farms near the village and made several stops on the return journey for the same purpose. At one village I was informed that some goats were dying from pneumonia. I started to make a postmortem on one and noticed a very enlarged spleen. I suspected anthrax, and so it was. The control measures were, of course, very different.

We visited the Suk in Mosul before catching the night train for Baghdad, where we arrived the next morning. Megan has a note, "Everything all right in the house, and it is nice to have good food again, but it is very hot, temperature 112."

By now there were fifteen in the FAO team, and with our Iraqi, American, and European friends, social life was interesting. When foreigners are gathered overseas they tend to be thrown together, and this sometimes makes for interesting contacts.

In Iraq one is constantly reminded of the historical significance of this part of the world. The ruins of Babylon are only fifty miles from Baghdad. On one visit there I picked up a piece of stone on which there is some cuneiform writing. It is one of my most treasured possessions. The friezes on the walls and the bulls and dragons on the Ishta gate, which were originally covered with brilliant enamel, indicate how beautiful the ancient city was. The Hanging Gardens were constructed like a ziggurat. The water was pumped up from wells in the foundation. This was in the time of Nebuchadnezzar. History reveals that he was not a tyrannical ruler. Jerusalem was not destroyed and the bulk of her population was not disturbed and so it might have remained had not the Jews stubbornly resumed their intrigues with Egypt. The prophet Jeremiah knew the futility of further revolt and did everything in his power to save his countrymen from rushing to disaster. "Serve the King of Babylon," he cried, "and live. Wherefore should this city be laid waste."

The museum is one of Baghdad's most famous attractions. Here are to be seen the wonderful objects found by Sir Leonard Woolley at Ur. This was the city built on the ruins of other cities, one of which was the home of Abraham twenty centuries before the time of Christ. Sir Leonard's collection is from the royal cemetery at Ur where he found the tombs of King A bar gi and Queen Shibad. He gives a picture of the tomb as it was 5,000 years ago: "The Queen herself deep in a wooden bier in a fantastic headdress of golden rings and beach leaves, her body covered with amulets and beads and a golden cup near her hand. None of the bodies showed any sign of violence." Sir Leonard suggests that the people may have been drugged. It seemed that they went to their deaths of their own free will in a ceremony that they believed would be a rapid transition from one world to the next.

Near Baghdad the Tigris becomes very low in the summer so that many small islands are formed in the middle of the river. Here hundreds of people make gardens and pitch tents in which they live. Also along the shore, Nile perch are cooked in the characteristic local fashion—split and skewered on sticks surrounding an open fire. One day Megan hired a boat and I rowed on this famous river. The Chaldeans, Babylonians, and the Assyrians were irrigation experts, and in their time the area between the Tigris and the Euphrates was part of the Fertile Crescent and the home of great civilizations. After the Mongol invasion of the thirteenth century, the great irrigation systems fell into ruin.

A short ride from Baghdad is the Arch of Ctesiphon, built by Cyrus the Great of Persia in 500 B.C. It is a remarkable engineering feat. The present ruins, which we visited several times, date from A.D. 300.

One day a man looking very much like Lawrence of Arabia came to the gate of the house. We invited him in and he had an interesting tale to tell while we were having tea. He said that he was now living in the desert with the Arabs and, with their aid, was experimenting with some agricultural crops. He described in detail how some crops would grow in the desert. It was a story that seemed to have some merit, and I suggested that he submit his ideas to the government. He also said that before and during the war he had been a pilot and with some others had been on the Stern gang list of those to be eliminated by the Jews. In order to get him out of danger the British had sent him to East Africa. I am sure this was not the whole story, but it was an example of the kind of thing one often encountered in that part of the world.

Our close friends were the Chadwicks, Major and Mrs., who had been in Iraq for thirty years—in fact since the end of the First World War. Chaddie was well known and well liked in the town. His wife, a former army nurse, was one of those lodged in the American embassy for several days in the 1941 uprising. One day we went with Chaddie to the R.A.F. base at Habaniah. There I did a rather unusual postmortem on a pig. It was held in the human mortuary. The condition turned out to be swine erysepelas with the typical vegetations on the heart valves. The causal organism of this disease may infect the skin of man.

We made another trip to the northern part of the country, this time staying at the railway rest house in Kurkuk. There was an oil field nearby then considered to be the largest in the world. Out in the desert were fires of burning gas, which had been alight since time immemorial and considered by some to be the fiery furnace of Shadrack, Meshack, and Abednigo of the Bible. We arranged to meet the veterinary personnel at one center, and when we entered the compound about ten young men stood up from a bench at the entrance. They looked smart and all had on clean white shirts. I said, "What do they do?" Nadjmi Deen said, "Nothing really. They're just friends of someone in authority." This was a good example of the nepotism that was prevalent there—perhaps it is no worse than the high unemployment that exists in Western countries at the present time.

Megan made some notes in her diary about this trip. She said: "Tuesday night we caught the 9 o'clock train for Kurkuk arriving there at 7:00 A.M. At the rest house there was a communal dining room which opened onto lovely lawns surrounded with flowers of every colour, roses, carnations, gladioli and lots of of others with a big hedge of oleander around the compound. One lawn had six iron beds on it ready for anyone who wanted to sleep out. We were invited to the British consul's house in the evening and he phoned to the next town, Suliemania, for the rest house to be ready for us.

"We hired a car for the trip to this Kurdish village perched on the side of a mountain with a view of the snow-capped Persian peaks in the distance. Again, we found the mountains of Northern Iraq to be very beautiful, with the background enhanced by the Kurds in their flowing robes, the men with sweeping pantaloons and curved daggers in their belts. There were no roads in the village. It was quite a reflief to get away from them! I was invited inside one of the houses but Frank was left outside. Sulimania is a primitive town of very narrow streets and mud huts, not a single Western type of shop. I do not think the locals see many Western people, judging by the way they stared.

I tried taking snaps of some small children, but they yelled so I gave up. I did get a snap of some young wives. They would not come out into the street for me so I signaled that I would like to go inside their courtyard. They opened the door for me. The husband was not there. I do not think he would have liked me in his hareem. The girls were very sweet and unspoiled. Later, from the veranda of the rest house, we watched some women at their prayers before they sat down around a big tray on the floor to eat their supper. It was the first time we had seen the women at prayer. The men, of course, go to their knees facing the East, even on the street, and touch the ground with their foreheads. At the Suk in the evening I bought some silver fox skins for about two shillings, 100 fils each. On the return trip to Kurkuk we saw the camel caravans again. There literally were hundreds of camels, all loaded. The chief of the tribe seemed happy to talk to us and have his picture taken."

In Baghdad we went again to live in the YMCA. It would soon be time to return to Rome and I was trying to bring to a conclusion some of the projects before leaving and before making preparations for the return journey. Megan made another trip to Babylon and was caught in a severe sandstorm in the desert. The road was not too good in those days, but she returned safely although the driver had some difficulty keeping in the tracks.

On the project we had made some considerable progress. Plans for the new laboratory had been completed, approved by the director and presented to the government. Much of the essential equipment had been ordered and some of it had arrived so that the laboratory could function reasonably well. Scientific literature was now reappearing on the library shelves. I had managed to select a student to send for further study at the London School of Tropical Medicine and actually saw him on the plane. This was not easy, since there was quite a lot of political competition for such an appointment.

One of the most important laboratory accomplishments had been to point out the importance of brucellosis to animal and human health, and to indicate some of the measures of prevention and eradication that should be taken. I suggested that Dr. G. Norman Hall, formerly a pathologist in Uganda and Nigeria, be my replacement. He arrived soon after I left and served two tours. The FAO project continued for several years.

One cannot leave Iraq without mention of Lawrence of Arabia, that romantic figure, and the great plan for an Arab nation in the Middle East after the War of 1918. The father of Lawrence was Sir Thomas Chapman, whose wife was a descendant of one of the Bengal governors and a Vansittart heiress. There were four daughters. Then came a Scottish governess into the picture. She was partly French and raised by a Calvinist minister's family on the island of Skye. In 1880 Sir Thomas eloped with the governess. He dropped the title and became Thomas Lawrence. T. E. was born in Tremadoc in North Wales. The house in which he was born is still there, and we called there a few years ago. He was the second of five sons. The first became a missionary in China near the Tibetan border. Their mother lived with him for many years. After T. E. was killed in a tragic motorcycle accident in England, Lady Astor, who was of course an American by birth and a prominent figure in England at that time, invited Mrs. Lawrence to live in a cottage on her estate. There she lived until she was nearly a hundred years old. Two younger brothers had been killed in the war. The youngest brother became a well-known archaeologist and a professor at London University. Prior to going to Oxford, T. E. was a student at a Jesuit School in France, although the whole family was Anglican. In Oxford he completed the four-year course in three years without apparently attending any lectures. During one extended holiday he spent the whole time touring the Middle East alone and on foot. Before he was twenty he was sending archaeological material back to the Asmmolean in Oxford. He learned Arabic and joined Leonard Woolley, who later excavated Ur.

In 1912 England signed a treaty which gave Germany control of the port of Alexandretta. Lawrence, a great student of history, went to see Kitchener about it in Cairo. Before war broke out, Woolley and Lawrence made a number of expeditions in the Middle East, including one across the Sinai Desert. At the age of twenty-six Lawrence had lived in Turkey, Syria, Palestine, Arabia, and Mesopotamia. He knew the history, language, customs, and topography of the area, and of course he was a friend of the people.

At the outbreak of WWI he was called to the military headquarters in Cairo. In 1915 the Hedjez Arabs revolted against the Turks after 400 years of Turkish domination. Ever since the decline of the Arabian Empire, many had tried to unify the people of Arabia. None were successful until Lawrence the unknown, the unbeliever, succeeded. The story of Lawrence's campaign is an unforgettable one. It is full of fascinating glimpses of Middle East history. For example, his fight in Petra was the first there since the time of the Crusades. In the last joint operation of the British and Arab forces, Allenby and Lawrence performed one of the most brilliant military operations in history. They lost less than 500 men in annihilating the Turkish forces, and captured 100,000 Turks. Lord Winterton observed that a noteworthy feature of the whole campaign was the personality of T. E. Lawrence. At times attacks are made by lesser minds on Lawrence's reputation and claims to fame. They ignore the regard felt for him by men of eminence who knew him, such as Churchill, Allenby, Shaw, Wavel, and Storrs. Megan and I knew Sir Ronald Storrs when he was governor of Cyprus. He had been civilian governor of Jerusalem following Allenby's victory and was a brilliant scholar of the Middle East.

During one of the many conferences held after the War of 1918 to try to settle the complicated Middle East question, Emir Faisal said that the new Arabian state should include all of Mesopotamia, Syria, and Palestine. At the same time he raised no objection to the Zionist proposal to encourage Jewish immigration into the country and to allow Jews to have full control of their schools, to establish a Jewish cultural center, and to participate in the government of Palestine: "Jews like ourselves are Semites and instead of relying on one of the great powers we should have the cooperation of the Jewish people for assistance in building up a great Semitic state. I appreciate fully Zionist aspirations. I understand the desire of the Jews to acquire a

Homeland, but so far as Palestine is concerned it must be Palestine subject to the rights and aspirations of the present possessors of the land."

If a joint Arab-Jewish state had been created *then* with a fair quota for immigrant Jews, how much more peaceful would the Middle East be today?

The time was approaching for our departure from Iraq, and we acquired some interesting artifacts such as silver items made by smiths working on the banks of the Tigris—where their ancestors had lived and worked for hundreds of years—and an antique copper vase that I found at Kashi's. Kashi sold Persian rugs and he taught me a lot about rugs and other things. Like other rug merchants, Kashi would let prospective buyers keep the rugs for weeks before they decided to purchase. I am afraid this was abused sometimes but it must have worked on the whole. The six rugs we bought from Kashi are still in the family, and after over thirty years they look more beautiful than ever.

We left Baghdad 6:00 A.M. on November 10, 1952. Our plane took us to Mafrac, which was really an R.A.F. landing strip in the desert. From there we went by car to Jerusalem. We spent some time in Amman. Here we visited the headquarters of the veterinary department. The prime minister of Jordan had some years previously qualified as a veterinarian at the Veterinary School of London University. Of course we stopped awhile on the shores of the Dead Sea, and somewhere on the way we visited an Arab refugee camp. This was an experience that I have not forgotten, and it strengthened my belief that a grave injustice was being done to the Palestine Arab.

In Jerusalem we lodged at the Saint Georges Hostel. This was the first of a number of enjoyable visits we made to this hospice. The city was divided into Arab and Jewish sides, separated by the Mendelbaum Gate. We were, of course, on the Arab side. We had time to see most of the historical sites and one evening I visited the Tomb in the Garden. For many years distinguished historians have considered that Christ was buried in this tomb and have produced much supporting evidence. After General Gordon left China he lived for a short time in Ain

Karim near Jerusalem. He explored the site of the tomb and found a grave that fulfilled the conditions of the biblical story. Seven years later the garden and grave were bought with contributions collected in Britain. The Garden Tomb (Jerusalem) Association now controls the area. The garden is obviously very old and the tomb fits the description of Jewish tombs of that time. There are two water cisterns of great age and a wine press sunk below the level of the ground; around it all lies the accumulated deposit of many centuries. Inside the tomb two crosses are engraved that date back to the seventh or sixth centuries. Outside on the surface of the tomb there is one incised cross of great age. The late Sir Flinders Petrie, a famous archaeologist who spent the last twenty years of his life in Jerusalem, said, "Jesus was crucified outside the Damascus Gate. The line of the third wall is proved; and that the date of the Garden Tomb is of the Herodian period." Alone I visited the garden at dusk one evening and was deeply impressed by the feeling of peace and tranquility there and the obvious signs of great antiquity.

From Jerusalem we flew to Beirut, and here met Egan, an FAO veterinary expert who had paid us a visit in Baghdad. We enjoyed lunch with him at the Saint Georges Club. The city was to face a bitter civil war in 1976.

We flew on to Cyprus in a DC-3. This plane had been a terrific war-horse in the past and even now there are a few still in use. We were met in Nicosia by Orhan who eighteen years previously had been my laboratory assistant and now was the chief veterinary officer. The veterinary laboratory and head office had changed little and were still located in the municipal gardens. We were reminded vividly of the time when the lab and other government buildings were burned down during the disturbances of 1932. Megan and I stirred up some other more pleasant memories by just walking along the streets of Nicosia. We called at Government House and at church met Mrs. Wright, the governor's wife, who had been a friend of ours during our 1930-34 tour.

In Rome I completed my final report before retiring from the FAO. An interesting point was that apart from the report

The odyssey begins here, in Staffordshire, England. My son, Bill, is standing in front of Weeford Church, where many of the Manleys lie buried.

Ugandan country girls. In 1925, a recent graduate of the Veterinary School of Liverpool University, I received an appointment from the Colonial Office to serve in Uganda. Uganda then seemed incredibly distant to me, but by 1927, when this photo was taken, I had become accustomed to the sights of the land.

Mombasa Cathedral, Kenya, whe
Megan and I were married
1927. Fifty years later we ce
brated our Golden Wedding Anr
versary.

*ere I am leaning against a road
gn in Uganda. In 1927 it took
ne month to make the journey
om London to East Africa, and
avel within that area was often
st as arduous.* Right: *Megan and
with one of my colleagues (sit-
ig on fender), prepare to chal-
ige the roads of Uganda in my
hevy. Let's see . . . only 460
ometers to Juba!*

Cyprus Veterinary Office after the riots of
1932. As veterinary research officer in
Cyprus, my main problem was finding an
anthrax vaccine. But there were political
problems as well. Riots against the British
forced the deportation of the bishop of
Kyrenia and the suspension of the Legislative
Council.

Left: *My Morris-Oxford,
which I brought to Nigeria
in 1928. Fine automobiles
have always held a special
attraction for me.* Above:
*My Morris-Cowley in
North Wales.*

Sir Winston Churchill's cow, presented to him by the Jersey (U.K.) government at war's end. I was in charge of the quarantine station at the dock, so my picture appeared, with the cow, in the London press.

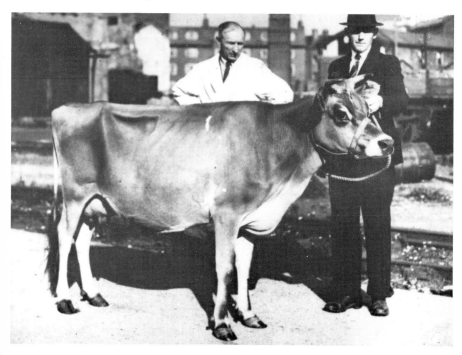

The ruins of Coventry Cathedral. We left Cyprus for Britain just when the war was starting. I worked for the Ministry of Agriculture during the London Blitz. Note the cross in the foreground, which stood fast against the Luftwaffe bombs that virtually destroyed the cathedral.

The difference between two worlds—a road sign in Iraq. In 1951 the Food and Agricultural Organization of the United Nations invited me to assume the post of veterinary microbiologist to the Iraq government.

Sir John Troutbeck, British ambassador to Iraq, and his wife welcome Megan and me shortly after our arrival.

Below: *Arab caravan.* Above: *Nomads in Baghdad. Both were familiar sights during my stay in Iraq.*

The Assyrian waiters of the Baghdad YMCA. The YMCA was our home for most of our stay in Iraq.

Our close friends Major and Mrs. Chadwick, left foreground, with the Prince Regent holding camera, and the king of Iraq, Faisal II. This photo was taken in 1953, five years before the assassination of Faisal by Arab nationalist rebels.

that went to the Iraq Government, I was asked to submit a confidential report. In this one could be less discreet. Sir Thomas Dalling was the FAO consultant in Rome and together we made a recording for the BBC dealing with the program in Iraq. For our flight to London we were fortunate to get seats on a Comet. This was our first jet flight and it was a thrill. The flight then took just over two hours. Soon after this the plane was grounded, apparently due to some kind of metal fatigue. Britain lost its ascendancy in jet flight at that time.

My parents who lived in London were senior citizens and were faced with some serious medical problems. My father had lived an exemplary life but partly because of the war had saved little money. I have always been grateful to the National Health Service in Britain. My parents were well taken care of. Nursing care and help was provided in the home to my parents during the last years of their lives, and expert help was always at hand. In the jet age, an age when families are scattered, this has become important. Our son now lives in Tehran—eleven thousand miles from our present home in California. We try to meet once a year in England.

On our arrival in London we were met by Dr. Dabbagh, whose course of study I had arranged prior to leaving Baghdad. He came to see us off at the air terminal at Victoria. Megan and I missed the bus, apparently because I delayed somewhat in the mens room. However the takeoff from Heathrow was delayed because it was a rough, snowy, and stormy night. This was a clipper flight and we slept in bunks. Owing to the weather we came down first in Shannon in Southern Ireland. Then against a headwind, we put down in Gander, Newfoundland, before finally arriving in New York. It had been a long flight. After paying the landing tax we found that we were without American money. However Bill was there to rescue us. We spotted him in the crowd by the old Epsom scarf he was wearing. We remained in New York for several days. Bill's theatre bookings this time were for *Madame Butterfly* and *South Pacific*. It was now the Christmas holiday and Bill came with us to Auburn.

8

U.S.A. INTERLUDE

The type of student at Auburn was now changing. No longer were they predominantly ex-service men but rather young people just out of school. Life in Auburn continued to be very enjoyable. The university life suited me very well, but as will be seen I was not fated to enjoy it for long. I continued as faculty adviser to the foreign students and to the International Club Committee. One interesting debate was between an Israeli and a Palestine Arab, the latter having lost his home in Jerusalem. Having just returned from the Middle East and visits to Arab refugee camps, my sympathies were perhaps not unnaturally with the Arab student.

Early in 1954 I started to raise broilers on a two-acre piece of land that we had bought on the edge of town. The idea was to buy 3,000 chicks and keep them for nine weeks. I did most of the work myself, going out every morning before starting work at the university at 8:00 A.M. Megan helped of course. It was interesting and instructive, particularly since I was teaching a course in poultry diseases and used the place for demonstration purposes. We planned later to build a house on the land.

Bill had joined the army partly to get his cumpulsory service over. At the time the country was desperately short of engineers, and Bill seemed to be mainly occupied in washing army dishes. I became rather frustrated with the situation and informed Senator Sparkman, whom we had met in Washington. Almost immediately Bill was offered a commission but by them he was en route to Japan. In Seatle he visited General Pick of Burma Road fame, who had been our neighbor in Auburn. Bill left for Japan on May 27, and about the same time Joan's baby daughter was born in Tampa.

83

We now planned to attend the World Poultry Congress in Edinburgh. We flew from Atlanta to New York in a Constellation and then boarded the *Queen Elizabeth* for Southampton. From there we went by bus to Winchester and had lunch at the Minster cafe, which overlooks the grounds of the historic cathedral. The whole reminded us of our wartime days there. We found Edinburgh cold after Alabama, and the warmest place in our residential hotel was the bathroom where there were some hot water pipes. We enjoyed seeing the famous Tattoo at the castle from where in the distance we could see the tiny island of Inchmickory, where I was stationed in the First World War.

After returning to Auburn we bought a car from Major Jones, a Welshman who said that he was born in New York and that for the first few years of his life spoke only Welsh. The car we bought from him finished up in Israel.

Early in 1955 we decided to build our house. Water supply was the problem, but after failing to get enough from a rather expensive drilling, we found that the city was going to supply the area. I myself planted over 100 pine trees and a large area of zoysia grass, which had to be sprigged into the ground. A few weeks after we had moved into the new home, Dean Sugg informed me that he had given my name to Paul Orvis, who was recruiting experts for the American Overseas Mission in Israel. This was aided by the Rockefeller Foundation at the State University of New York.

9

ISRAEL

Although we had only recently moved into the new house, I was keen on the Israel assignment and accepted the offer of a two-year appointment. Bill was on the way home from Japan, and we delayed our departure until he arrived and was released from the army. He had entered the Graduate School at Berkeley but was not due there until autumn, so he decided to come to Israel with us. Having shipped all our household belongings, we left Auburn in the Buick we were taking with us. I dropped off at Atlanta to visit the Communicable Disease Center and then flew to Washington, ostensibly for briefing. I was sent to the Israel desk. My mentor had never been to the Middle East. After four years in Cyprus and one in Iraq, I thought I was something of an expert! At least I had made a close study of the area. We had a pleasant flight from New York. We visited members of the family in London and Wales, and Bill visited his old school in Epsom. We flew to Rome in a turbojet, a Viscount, a fairly new plane at that time. I had requested accommodations at a reasonably priced hotel. They put us up in the Grand Palace! This was a bit too much for our tastes and the next day we moved into the Anglo American, where we had stayed in 1952. We once again visited Saint Peter's and some of the other famous sites, and it was pleasant to be able to show Bill some of the scenes that we knew so well. Of course, we visited the FAO headquarters to meet old friends. We were beginning to know and love Rome. Little did we think that we would return as refugees from Israel to spend many months there.

We arrived in Israel at 5:00 A.M. on the first of July and were met by Marshall Wiley, the legal adviser to the SUNY project. We were lodged at the Ramat Aviv Hotel, a pleasant place with separate cottages and a pool. The management impressed upon us how honest everyone was in the area, but it was not long before we realized that most valuables and especially radio sets had to be tied down or they would disappear. In view of what happened later on during our tour, and of course the very great place the Middle East has taken in the history of the world, some observations on the more important events that have taken place in my own lifetime might be of interest. However, before we deal with the end of Turkish jurisdiction in the Middle East in 1918, at the end of the war and the defeat of the Turks by General Allenby, let us take a glimpse into the past.

Four thousand years ago Jerusalem, under another name, was the chief city of the Canaanites. About 2,000 B.C. Abraham arrived in the area of Beersheba from Ur. In an Egyptian letter of the time there is a record that Palestine was being overrun by the Habiru. This may refer to the Hebrews. But the government at Jerusalem was in the hands of the Jebusites. At about 1,000 B.C. David was the ruler of the area from Dan to Beersheba. This was the largest extent of the Jewish domain. The reign of Solomon extended from 965 to 928. The palace and first temple were built. Trade routes to Mesopotamia, Asia Minor, and Africa were established. After Solomon, the kingdom was divided into Judah and Israel. Then came the time of the great prophets Elijah and Elisha, then Isaiah and Jeremiah. The kingdom of Israel ended with the invasion by the Assyrians in 723. Nebuchadnezzar conquered Jerusalem and many of the inhabitants were taken prisoner to Babylon. After the Persian conquest the Jews were allowed to return by Cyrus the Great. Many of them remained behind. It is interesting to note that, until recent times, there was a large Jewish population living peacefully in Baghdad. Then came Alexander the Great, followed by the Romans. Apart from the great revolt of A.D. 66, the Jews ruled no longer in Jerusalem. Constantine, the first Christian emperor, occupied Palestine and with his mother, Helena, began transforming it into a Christian city. There was another short Persian invasion to be followed by the Arab conquest. Abd el Malik built the Dome of the Rock, which still remains one of the most beautiful and dominant historical monuments in the area. In 969 the Egyptians ruled, to be followed in 1077 by the Turks. For nearly 200 years the Crusaders were fighting in Palestine, and for a time a Latin kingdom was established in Jerusalem.

As I mentioned earlier, the Turkish era ended with the arrival of the British under General Allenby. During the war, Colonel Gilbert Clayton, in charge of Egyptian military intelligence, and Wyndham Deeds, intelligence officer from Gallipoli, put together the Arab League. Clayton was encouraged by High Commissioner Sir Henry McMahon. The Arab League became an organization resembling the CIA. The object was to supplant Turkish influence in the Middle East and at the same time foster an Arabic world in the area. Lawrence was the frankest in declaring the purpose of the Cairo band. At the time Chaim Weizmann was fostering the Zionist cause, Clayton and some members of the British government in London had many meetings with Faisal, Weizmann, and others to consider the future of the area. Copies of the official correspondence of the time make for fascinating reading. The Zionist Commission, with Weizmann at its head, arrived in Palestine. Britain was trying to assure its position in the Middle East for the future and to show support for the Arab and Jewish aspirations at the same time—a difficult and, as it proved, an almost impossible task.

The Balfour letter and the Sykes-Picot agreement were documents on which the Zionists and the Arabs put much faith and which led to much misunderstanding. For example, the so-called Syrian Welfare Committee in Cairo, which represented Arab nationalist opinion, addressed a letter to Sykes that summed up their understanding of Zionist intentions. They stated, "We clearly deduce from your letter that all the Zionists demand is liberty for the Jews to settle in our country and to enjoy full civil rights." They added that they had received a similar explanation from General Clayton. This was the beginning of the trouble. The British presented the Arabs with a rosy image of Zionists' intentions and at the same time urged Weizmann to pursue a policy of caution. Behind the scene was the hope of getting the Turks away from their alliance with Germany.

Britain received a mandate over Palestine after the war. The Jewish population was small. Soon after the mandate it rose to 30,000. After 1933 it rose to 60,000, due mainly to refugees from Germany.

The Zionists under the mandate utilized the period to lay the foundations for the Jewish State. The Jewish community had an elected assembly with limited rights of self-government. The state of Israel, which eventually emerged, was based on this state within a state. The rising numbers of Jewish emigrants came largely from Germany. Time and time again the Arabs demanded an end to Jewish emigration and a halt to land sales to the Jews. Several schemes for the partition of the country were made, but the Arabs believed, I think rightly, that their homeland was being taken away. Finally the British government, unable to find a solution to the Palestine problem, asked the United Nations to take over the dispute. Violence broke out. Britain ended its mandate and the Zionists proclaimed the state of Israel. The American government was the first to recognize the new state. Washington has consistently given much military and economic aid. The Arabs believe that this has robbed them of Palestine and has put to flight nearly a million Palestinians.

It can be seen that the Middle East was a complicated picture that became aggravated with the flood of refugees from the war in Europe. This whole situation played into the hands of the Zionists. Sadly enough, the saving of the Jewish refugees led to the desperate Arab refugee problem.

One of the first impressions we had in Tel Aviv was the existence of military conscription and the large number of women that seemed to be in the army. Our SUNY group was housed in an office building within walking distance of the veterinary laboratory where I was working. The director of the laboratory was overseas, and there did not seem to be anyone with enough authority to let me start to work. In fact, it was some days before I could get a chair and desk. This went on for several weeks and was very frustrating. Apparently, the director was much feared. However, he eventually returned and things began to move. I was asked to study the various laboratory departments in turn and report on them. I was assigned a very small laboratory and two young veterinarians were posted to me for training. Dr. Moscona was a graduate of Toulouse, and the other, Dr. Baroutchieva, was from Sophia. Later, Dr. Pearlstein of Zurich was added.

In my report on the department of milk hygiene, I indicated that a satisfactory method of carrying out the examination of milk samples for mastitis infection was being followed. This was aided by the fact that Israel is a small country with a large number of veterinarians and thus is able to institute efficient control measures. However, at that time methods of milk production in the field were in urgent need of attention from the point of cleanliness.

Dr. Radin, in charge of the Department of Bacteriology of Meat, has had the advantage of working with Dr. A. Jepson— an expert in the field both here and in Denmark. An interesting point about species identification is that bovine, equine, and camel sera were being used. It was noted that frozen fish was being imported from Poland, Norway, and Germany, and also that bovine mouth parts and feet were being imported. This latter seemed very undesirable with the possibility of foot and mouth disease being present in the country of origin. In the serological department, tests were being made for brucellosis, dourine, and salmonella. The techniques were being well carried out, but more veterinary supervision was needed, and working conditions were not good, to say the least. In fact, I marveled at how sophisticated techniques were being carried out under what seemed to be a lack of cleanliness in the whole laboratory in Tel Aviv. However, it was expected that these conditions would be corrected at the new laboratory at Beit Dagon.

I was able to continue my interest in brucellosis by working on the Milk Ring Diagnostic Test and the plate test. It was again shown that the Ring Test gave false positive results with milk from drying off cows. Literature indicated that the test in sheep and goats was not satisfactory owing to irregularity of distribution of the stained antigen. Some plate tests on sheep indicated that the ring test might eliminate this problem and that it might have some value as a screening test. This work was interrupted by the outbreak of hostilities in 1956.

We were fortunate in soon finding a partially furnished house in Ramat Gan, a suburb of Tel Aviv. The street was named McDonald, after a former American ambassador, and the house of the then Ambassador Larkin was directly across the street from ours. In fact, the official guard spent most of the time on our gate, perhaps because of the frequent cups of tea available. Before we actually moved into the house we made several trips into the country with Bill, including one to the Jewish side of Jerusalem. After this, Bill caught a Turkish ship from Haifa to Istanbul and then went across Europe by bus. He had registered in the Graduate School of Physics at Berkeley.

Our furniture and the car arrived safely and we were looking forward to an interesting and rewarding tour. There were a large number of experts in the AID program and about twenty in the SUNY section. Many of the staff lived in a large apartment complex. This, some of us felt, was a mistake, since it, to some extent, isolated these people from the people of the country. In fact the building became known as the American kibbutz.

One of the experts imported a very large Cadillac, which he always parked in a prominent position. This did not seem to be a good way to make friends in a developing country, but the owner, an aggressive type, insisted that this was the way to show the natives what American business methods could do. Some years later I believe he died from too much alcohol.

Christian churches and missions are, of course, scattered throughout the country. We attended the Church of England Mission in Jaffa. Only a handful of Western Christians attended. We knew the Reverend Mr. Allison and his wife well. Later in Addis Ababa we met his brother, the bishop of Khartoum. There were five Allison brothers, all in the Church. One Sunday I had the pleasure of reading the lesson in Jaffa, perhaps one of the oldest settlements in Israel. The Jews were making it difficult for

Allison to get reading material for his mission, and some months after we left Israel we heard that one of his lady helpers had been expelled from the country. Allison was later transferred to Jerusalem.

One evening Megan and I were invited to the British consul general's in Jerusalem for dinner. The consul mentioned that he had been trying to locate a Richard Hughes, who had lived in Jerusalem for many years. Megan said, "He is my uncle!" Apparently he had owned a lot of property in and around the city. He had passed on and the consul had been trying to get in touch with a member of the family for many months since much of the property had been taken over by the Jews. The upshot of the conversation was that the consul said he would send a letter from Megan to a judge on the other side through the Mendelbaum Gate. Megan received a charming letter from the judge saying that the late Mr. Hughes had been one of his dearest friends and offered to help in finding some of the confiscated property. However, we were soon evacuated and there seemed to be little we could do in later years.

One day in Ramat Gan we were attending a social at the Lawn Bowling Club. The British ambassador and I were invited to play and this we did, in our stocking feet. Since that time Megan and I have played in Rhodesia, Kenya, and the United States. Last year in Riverside we played against Wales. The game has an international flavor and Australia and New Zealand, South Africa, and of course, Great Britain are very keen on it. The story goes that Admiral Drake was playing bowls on Plymouth Hoe when the Spaniards Armada was sighted in the Channel. He said, "Let us finish the game first."

A few miles north of Tel Aviv on the coast was Hertseliya, with beautiful beaches. At that time it was not too crowded and we spent many happy hours there. One day further up the coast we had to leave our car at the top of a small cliff. We changed up there and I rather foolishly left my shorts and watch in the car. When we returned from our swim my watch and shorts were missing. A friend of mine who lived nearby loaned me his shorts, which were several sizes too large. So I reported the loss to the local police station but heard nothing further.

This coast of Israel is studded with the remains of Roman, Crusader, and Moslem occupation. One can still pick up Roman coins on the beaches.

The Israeli Symphony had just been started and one night we heard Yehudi Menuhen. Strange that he decided to settle and founded a school in London. Another pleasant evening was when Dame Sybil Thorndyke and her husband, whom we met, gave a Shakespeare recital. We never forgot her performance in *Macbeth*.

A few miles on the Tel Aviv-Jerusalem road is the town of Ramla with an ancient mosque and Crusader ruins. While exploring some of the latter, I lost my car keys. However, some Israeli ex-soldiers came along and said they could start any car, and this they did using a bit of wire and some silver paper from a cigarette carton. Nearby Beersheba was a small, Arab village when we were there, and market day was interesting. Camels were being sent to Tel Aviv for slaughter for food.

Some time before we left the U.S.A., I received some literature from a Canadian oil company saying that they were drilling in Israel. I bought some shares and I think to my surprise found out that it was a genuine outfit. The well was called King David No. 1. Megan and I often went out to watch the work. They found no oil but another company drilling nearby did!

In midsummer we visited Britain to see our respective families, and I was able to consult with several research institutes, such as the Medical Research Center at Mill Hill, the Lister Institute, the National Institute for Dairying at Reading, and, of course, the Ministry of Agriculture Veterinary Laboratory in Weybridge. In our many visits to Britain we usually hire a car in London and go by road through the West Midlands to Wales, often including Stratford and the Cotswolds in our route. We returned to Israel via Rome, where we had time to visit some of our old haunts. It was a typically hot summer day in Rome, and we spent a couple of hours riding around in a carriage with our shoes off.

We had by now visited most of the important historical sites in Israel, and one day in Jerusalem we went to a service in the large Jewish Orthodox synagogue. This was a very interesting experience. The women were separate from the men and were in a sort of balcony. Jewish and Arabic music are both largely pitched in the minor key and bear some similarity to each other.

Nazareth was our favorite part of the country, and we made a number of visits there. We were there at Christmas time in 1955. We went to a Baptist mission church one evening and were amazed to find that all the congregation were Arabs. One of the interesting sites is Mary's Well, particularly since it is still the only source of water for the city. One of my best color slides is one of Nazareth, in which I have a church, a mosque, and a synagogue in the same field with a dramatic background of a stormy sky. We returned there again at Easter time. The Sunday service was given by a Christian Arab. We also liked the lake-shore and managed to get a beautiful picture of the fishermen's nets hanging out to dry. While in the north we visited the kibbutz at Endor. Bible students will remember the Witch of Endor. A kibbutz is, of course, a communal settlement. They were, I think, started in Israel by the Russian Jews. Some people can live in a kibbutz all their lives; others do not like the life and leave. The layout of a kibbutz is in the form of a wagon wheel. Quite often this form is followed so that they can make a very good defense post, especially if properly located. Near Carmel we visited Elijah's Cave and also a Druse village, where we were lucky enough to see a wedding. The Druse is a small sect that originated from the Moslems.

The work was now going quite well. Diagnostic material came into the laboratory, and this was used by my students in the training program. I became friends with Dr. van der Hoeden, a Dutch scientist, who was working on leptospirosis at the Biological Institute at Ness Ziona. He subsequently wrote an important text-book on the subject. His son was teaching in a kibbutz and apparently had no desire to return to the outside world.

Reservists were being called up by the military and it was obvious that something was afoot. However, it was a complete surprise when one night Marshall Wiley, our young legal adviser, called at the house and told us to pack two suitcases, for we would be leaving in a few hours. Most of the American personnel were being evacuated. Britain, France, and Israel were apparently at war with Egypt. We were going to run away and leave much of our worldly belongings behind. Two things we had to take— the silver candelabra and the income tax papers! We were not happy about leaving, especially since our friend, Wing Commander Bishop, the British air attaché, said he was not leaving. However, early in the morning we left for Lod airport. Only the women were going on this flight. Tommy Thompson and his wife were there. We could see nobody else we knew. The flight was delayed for several hours waiting for women and children coming in from all over Israel. Finally the pilot signaled that he had to leave. Apparently there was room for one more on board, so I threw my car keys to an embassy driver and joined the ladies. We were headed for Munich. We arrived in Munich late at night in a severe snowstorm. We circled the area for an hour before we could get down. Our refugees were met by members of the American community and Megan and I were taken in by the administration officer. We remained in Munich for ten days, waiting to find out if and where we would be posted. We were well taken care of and received P.X. privileges. We sent cables to the children, telling them that we were O.K. and made arrangements to receive some money. It was very cold in Munich compared to Israel, and the administrative officer loaned me his "teddy bear" overcoat, which was two sizes too big for me. I visited the Munich Veterinary College, one of the oldest in Europe, and in a different mood went to the famous beer cellar, which used to be patronized by Hitler.

We also went to the Deutschmuseum to hear the *Stabat Mater*. We had heard the soprano, whose name escapes me, in Israel. She was so small that she had to stand on a box which was suitably disguised, of course.

After many rumors, we were finally posted to Rome with a number of our friends, including the Birdsalls of New York, McMenamy from Montana, and Mays. Mays had been information officer in Israel and was married to an Englishwoman. With others we were allotted a room in the embassy on the Via Veneto—a famous street. Here we met daily to discuss our fate and to collect our mail. Megan and I found accommodation at the Majestic Hotel, a very pleasant place near the Borghese Gardens.

One of the first things we had to do while in Rome was to visit Naples in order to get a visa for Megan. It gave us the opportunity to see Vesuvius once again—this time from land.

It is interesting to look at the basis for the 1956 war, in which we were somewhat remotely involved. The following notes are from the *Memoirs of David Ben-Gurion,* published in 1970:

July 1954

The British announce their intention of departing from the Suez Canal Zone. The pullout results in the Lavon affair. The affair begins when the Egyptians uncover an Israeli Secret Service plot to start a wave of terrorism in Cairo and Alexandria that can be attributed to a local organization called the Moslem Brotherhood. The idea is to prove the weakness and incapacity to govern of the Egyptian authorities and thus persuade the British to remain in the Canal Zone. The plot is revealed by an Israeli double agent. Arrests are made and two men are subsequently hanged. Subsequent investigation reveals possible complicity of Defense Minister Lavon under whose nominal control the Secret Service operates and who is known for his belligerent attitude towards Egypt. Lavon denies all knowledge of the plot but quietly resigns from the government.

1955

Ben-Gurion embarks on a search for alliances for Israel. Attempts to interest Americans in guaranteeing the country's security in return for strategic bases.

Meanwhile with the departure of the British from the Suez,

the U.S.S.R. shifts its policy and becomes the champion of Arab nationalism.

July 1956

Egypt nationalizes the Canal, taking control away from the British French consortium.

October 1956

Ben-Gurion participates in a secret conference with the British and French at Sevres, France. He agrees to a combined military operation whereby Israel will move to oust the Egyptians from the trouble spots of Gaza and the Straits of Tiran. The British and French will then intervene by parachuting into the Canal Zone ostensibly to make a buffer zone between Egypt and Israel. Early in November the United States and Russia denounced the intervention and the British and French pulled out. The U.N. troops occupied Gaza.

Although the war was soon over, there was no suggestion from the U.S. authorities in Israel that our group would be soon returning. We were informed that our belongings were safe and were being taken care of. Some of the group were now being assigned to other parts of the world, and it was interesting to wonder each day where one might be sent.

I was asked by the agricultural attaché to make a survey of poultry diseases in Italy, and this I attempted to do. It was a large undertaking, especially since there was little money for travel expenses. However, I was able to meet a number of Italian veterinarians, including Dr. Fontanelli of the Rome laboratory. We also renewed our acquaintance with our former colleagues at the FAO.

We met June Laverick, a very young movie star from England, and became friends with her. In later years she became quite famous. One night at our hotel our waiter taught her the Italian way to eat spaghetti, and another evening with Marshall Wiley we had a pleasant time out at one of Rome's famous restaurants. June was very home-loving and often talked about her "mum" back home in her Yorkshire Pub. June returned to the same Yorkshire town when she retired. Another man we met often was a well-known Australian opera singer. He was a real type with a large overcoat with a fur collar. He used to buy good Italian bread, cheese, and wine and often brought it to our room for lunch. He knew Rome well and was a fund of knowledge about its ancient churches. We too were coming to know the city well and had tramped over most of the streets in at least the center of the city.

There was a hint that we might be sent to Spain but this came to nothing. Finally the news came that some of us were being posted to Ethiopia. After having our medicals, Megan and I set off for a trip to Florence, returning via Perugia and Assisi. At Perugia I received a message from the embassy saying that my medical report was not right—would I please hurry back? Apparently some of the laboratory tests were not good so I was sent for reexamination. The clinical examination was again satisfactory but the lab tests not so. This was repeated again, much to my discomfort, but the clinical finally prevailed. So we were ready for Ethiopia. Before leaving we had the opportunity of meeting Clare Luce, who was then the American ambassador in Rome.

Very few of our group from Israel were now left. We arrived in Ethiopia to find the red carpet out at the airport. Alas, it was not for us. A few minutes after we arrived another plane came in and we saw Richard Nixon and his wife descend. He was then vice president—and now?

Bud Molohon, the chief of the Agricultural Division, met us and we spent the night at his house. I remember that we had some Ethiopian venison for dinner. The next day we moved into the Ghion Hotel, where we remained for two months until we returned to Israel.

I was to work in the veterinary laboratory. The only other qualified veterinarian was Dr. Poppe from Germany, working for the FAO. One of the jobs we had to do was to test the emperor's cattle for tuberculosis. They had been tested before but the reactors had not been removed. I can remember that Kesteven, the veterinary chief with FAO in Rome, had told me that he had flown out to try to get something done about it. We still found some reactors but I do not know what happened to them. Poppe went on leave to Kenya and so I was left in charge. The main work of the laboratory was the preparation of vaccines against bovine pleuropneumonia and rinderpest. The techniques had been well established, so there was no real problem. The chief veterinary officer was not a qualified man and in fact only appeared about once a week. My immediate assistant was a typical Ethiopian called Affiworke. He had slim, delicate features and a physique much like certain Egyptians, and I enjoyed working with him. I was allowed the use of a car, an ancient Mercedes diesel, with a driver. He was a pleasant man but was often slightly intoxicated. I gave him one of my old suits in which he proudly appeared the very next day.

One night we were at the theater when the emperor and empress were present. One Sunday the church service was conducted by the bishop of Khartoum. Imagine our surprise when we found that the bishop was the brother of the Reverend Mr. Allison from Tel Aviv, whom we knew so well.

We left Addis on March 11, on Ethiopian Airlines. Crossing the equator we were each given a certificate. I recalled when I had first crossed it by ship, going to Kenya in 1926. We were now going by plane to Israel via Nairobi. We were held up in the latter place for several days, and Megan and I were delighted since it was in Mombasa that we had been married in 1927. We met the Waterers and Natrass, old friends from our Cyprus days. Waterer was the chief forestry officer and Natrass the government mycologist. We also met Polding, a fellow worker on brucellosis who had visited us in Auburn. We stayed at the well-known New Stanley Hotel with the famous Thorn Tree Sidewalk Cafe—a wonderful place to see the world go by! There was only one other hotel of any size in Nairobi at that time, namely the Norfolk.

Megan and I decided to visit Uganda, where we spent our

first tour overseas. This was before the days of General Amin and Uganda was then an easy place to visit. We went by train to Tororo, not far across the Kenya border. There we hired a car and toured the Bukedi District, where I had been veterinary officer many years before. We went to Mbale, which had been my headquarters, and found the small hospital where Joan had been born. It still looked like a shed with a tin roof. We also visited the church where Joan had been the first white baby to be christened. After some searching the African curate found a book of church records of christenings and there was Joan's name—the first in the book. Then we tried to find the camp at Kalait, where Megan and I had spent nearly three months under canvas. We called at one *shamba* and the owner came out to speak to us. After a while he said, "I remember you. You taught me how to play soccer when I was about eight years old." I did remember playing with some small boys around the camp and have an old snapshot of a group of them, including this fellow. Then he said, "I have been working for the veterinary department and now I am retired. I have two wives and a small farm." His seemed to be a very peaceful and happy sort of life. Before returning to Nairobi we went as far as Mjanji and saw once again Lake Victoria, where we had so many interesting times in the early days.

We left Nairobi on May 25, after what had been for Megan and me a memorable visit. Before boarding the plane Thompson and I took some good lion pictures.

We were off the plane late that night in Djibouti. It was a typically hot and humid Red Sea night. Early the next morning Marshall Wiley met us in Tel Aviv, and we made directly to the Ramat Aviv hotel. Our furniture, or most of it, had been returned to our house on McDonald Street, and some time was spent checking with the house agent, Mr. Greenbaum, and also seeing that our car was all right. At the laboratory there was much to do in preparing a final report and inspecting the new facilities at Beit Dagon.

It had been a strange tour with a slow start and interruption by the war. However, it had been full of interest for Megan and me. It was interesting comparing notes with old friends. Some, of course, had returned directly to the U.S.A., and we did not see them again. Some had got as far as India. There were many welcome back parties and visits to favorite spots, such as the beach at Hertseliya. We were particularly pleased to see, once again, the Bishops and the Allisons who, of course, had not left. I doubt if our exodus was really necessary, but it was a wonderful experience to spend many months in Rome and Addis, and to return once again to Uganda and Kenya.

We left Tel Aviv on June 28. There was a nice crowd to see us off. However, with the passing of my father, it was a rather sad return to London. We were reunited with the Birdsalls, who had been with us on our travels. They were heading for a visit to the village of Birdsall in Yorkshire. We had a good flight back via Manchester to New York and then on to Washington.

The McMenamies were there and Bart and I went to the ICA office. I inquired about the jobs in India and Ethiopia. They said they had no record of the Ethiopian appointment, but later Marshall Wiley, our lawyer, confirmed that they had made the offer by cable to Addis Ababa. They also confirmed that they had approved my appointment to India and were waiting on the final approval from that country. I visited the government laboratories at Beltsvile. This was where Buck and Cotton had done the original work on Strain 19 Vaccine against brucellosis.

10

U.S.A. AGAIN

We then left for California where Bill had an apartment in Beverly Hills. After an unsuccessful attempt at breaking into the movies, he was working with the Litton engineering company. He had been on one T.V. show with Lady Lawton and was in a number of amateur shows in Hollywood, but I do not think he employed an agent!

We met two ex-G.I.s from wartime days—Dick Thatcher, now a prominent lawyer, and Jerry Wesler, the owner of a prospering burlap factory. We also had pleasant evening with the Janisens, from Tel Aviv. I sat for the California Civil Service Examination. We then all flew to Tampa to see Joan. Her husband, Gordon, was at McDill Air Base.

After a few days we bought a car and headed for Auburn. I still had not heard from Washington, and I was getting anxious about the job situation. It seemed that now was another turning point in my life. My old job in Auburn had been filled. Eventually we heard that India or someone out there had refused to confirm my appointment. After having been picked by the University of Missouri and approved by Washington, this seemed very strange, and, of course, I never found out the reason. I had turned down a job at the University of Florida, and it was now late in the season for university recruitment. However, I heard that I had passed the California examination and so I joined the department of Agriculture there in the Poultry Inspection Department. Before leaving Auburn we had a number of pleasant social meetings with our friends—the Irvings, Kudernas, and Robertses, and Leibold, Showalter, Glyde, and Peet—all professors at the university.

We soon found an apartment on Elm Drive in Beverly Hills. It was pleasant in a way and Bill lived nearby. The job was routine and boring. We both missed our friends in the academic life. I did manage to take some courses at U.C.L.A., but the idea of going farming was strong. It is possibly a basic desire in the hearts of many men. We joined the Los Angeles Welsh Society and sometimes attended the Welsh Chapel. This gave Megan a good deal of pleasure. We also joined the Holmby Park Lawn Bowling Club. Megan attended a school training for T.V. work.

We bought two acres of land in Palmdale and so did Bill. The sales pitch was that, being close to the Edwards Air Base, the land had great potential—and so it seemed. It was a pleasant spot on the high desert and was dotted with Joshua trees. The anticipated development had not occurred after fifteen years and we sold out. It does seem probable that Los Angeles will soon develop a new airport in the area.

I used to attend meetings in various parts of the state, and one time Megan came with me to Sacramento. We were hit by another car that ran a red light. Megan was badly shaken up, and, although we were in a hotel in the middle of the city, I had great difficulty in getting medical attention.

One night in Los Angeles we went to hear Emlyn Williams, the Welsh actor, reading the works of Dylan Thomas; afterwards we had an interesting talk with him. After all, we all came from the same part of the world! Bill was with us. We also met Ralph Richardson after he performed at the Hollywood Bowl. Our previous meeting had been in Wales during the war. Bill and I went to hear Aneurin Bevan, the British Labor leader. Like many Welshmen he was a great orator.

One of Bill's friends was Lewis Marvin, who was trying to build a house on the top of a hill above Malibu. One day we drove up there with a young couple, Sophy and Jim Mellen, who had lived in Yugoslavia, where their father was in the diplomatic service. Near the top we saw a Lotus car hanging over a dangerous part of the track. We were worried about Marvin, but after walking up to the house—or rather the frame—we found that he was safe. On the way down we thought that Jim was having some trouble driving through the mist. No wonder—he had his contacts reversed!

We decided to buy a poultry farm—or at least I did. I do not think that Megan really approved. We decided on locating in Yucaipa, near Redlands. We liked Redlands, a small university town about sixty miles from Los Angeles and forty miles from Palm Springs. First we planned another visit to Britain. We went via Kokomo, Indiana. Joan's husband, Gordon, was now stationed at Bunker Hill Air Base. The train from Chicago was a bit primitive. The air conditioner was not working and there was water dripping from some overhead pipes. Our plane from Chicago to New York was grounded and we transferred to a Viscount turbojet. We were also delayed at Idlewild International Airport and our friends, the Birdsalls of the Israel days, came down from Albany. We had a nice time talking about our experiences in Israel, Rome, and Ethiopia. This time we flew via Gander to Prestwick and on to London in a Britannia plane.

As usual, we spent our time between London, the Midlands, and North Wales. This time we found Manley Village in Cheshire. This must have had some association with the family. The squire of the village, whom we met, was Mr. Gladstone, a grandson of the great Victorian statesman and prime minister. In North Wales we spent some time settling the remnants of my uncle's estate. Most of it had been left to charity. Our friend and colleague, Norman Hall, had now returned after working with FAO in Baghdad. He came up to town and we met at the Royal Commonwealth Society. We left London on July 5. Stanley Richards, Megan's cousin, took us out to the airport. He and his wife did this on a number of occasions. In New York we stayed at the Algonquin, a famous old hotel associated with the theater. We returned to California by way of Joan's place in Indiana. Although we did not arrive back in Los Angeles until 3:00 A.M., due to a delay caused by a snow storm, Bill was there to greet us.

After a few days rest we went to Yucaipa to start our farming experience. Megan has the following note in her diary: "Up at 6:00 A.M. No more late nights for the Manleys." How right she was! A week later she wrote: "Up at 5:00 A.M. . . . What a life!"

The egg ranch itself was comparatively small, 5,000 hens, but I was buying eggs from a number of other producers. I went in when egg prices were depressed and small producers were being eliminated, but I could see great potential ahead. One day a salesman from Los Angeles came in looking for a job. He seemed to know the business and I needed help. I bought a refrigerated truck and put a number of display cabinets in large markets. Business looked promising but as time went on I found that, in spite of a great deal of hard work, my bank balance was not improving and I could not pinpoint the trouble. Bill came over often and we usually put him to work!

On a different note, we joined the Redlands Lawn Bowling Club. We alternated our churchgoing between the Episcopal and the Christian Science churches. We were becoming interested in music again and joined the chorus on the Redlands Bowl. We sang in many operas there. I gave some lectures at the University of Redlands and found time to take some courses. Two of them were concerned with Africa and the Middle East. They were taught by Dr. Dittmar, with whom I became friends. His father had fled from Germany to escape Hitler.

At the end of April Bill brought a new girl over. Nothing new in that except that she was a Persian. Her name was Simine Attabay. She seemed very quiet and reserved and we liked her. It was sometime later that we found out that she was a niece of His Imperial Highness, the shah of Iran. In July she left for a visit to Paris to be with her aunt, Princess Aschraf, the twin sister of the shah. Princess Aschraf is a keen advocate of women's interests in the U.N. and elsewhere.

During the election in February we did some canvasing for the late John F. Kennedy. I believe his tragic passing has seriously damaged the morale of the American people and, even after fifteen years, the wound is still healing. Simine and Bill came over for Christmas and we had a very enjoyable time. David Linford, son of our friends from Tamworth, England, was studying and traveling in the U.S.A. and came to see us. One day we sent him out on the egg truck to the Mexican border. He is now a prominent builder in Europe.

The following year, 1961, we concentrated on trying to make a go of the farm. It was a very tough task and in spite of much effort, we thought that it was not going to be a successful venture. Before the end of the year we decided to give it up. Meanwhile, I had returned to my job in the Department of Agriculture.

The most interesting family news was that Joan and her husband were being stationed in England and would be there for three years. We went over to the air base in Indiana to see them before they left.

Back in Redlands, we took part in our first opera in the Redlands Bowl. It was *La Traviata*. Jimmy Guthrie, the director, was the son of a wealthy newspaper man in the valley. He was studying music in New York and fell in love with a beautiful and talented music student. Jimmy's father suggested that he should come home. This he did but he brought his bride with him. Megan and I sang in many operas in the Bowl, the leads being usually from the Metropolitan Opera House. Mrs. Guthrie gave a brilliant performance as the lead in *Turandot*. We had a very busy year in 1962. In the Bowl we were in *The Magic Flute, The Pirates of Penzance, La Forza del Destino,* and *Elijah*. The last was under the direction of Harold Farbman. At Christmastime we were in the *Messiah* chorus, as usual.

In July Simine left for a visit to Paris and Iran and later in the year Bill, Megan, and I left for England and France. We were to attend an international veterinary conference at Cambridge University. On arrival in London we hired a car and arrived in Cambridge at midnight. I think Bill was surprised to find that the festivities were still going on. We met many interesting delegates from different countries in Europe and Bill enjoyed being in the famous and beautiful city in which he had been born.

We then returned to Joan's place in Fairford. This is the base from which the original Concorde, that is, the British version, took off. Bill headed for Paris and we soon followed. There we met our old friends, Mays and his wife. He was now the information officer at the American embassy. He had been with us in Israel and Rome. We stayed with the Mayses in the suburb of

Vicinet. We also met Simine and Bill. After we returned to
England Bill bought two antique cars, one a 1934 Lagonda and
the other a 1927 Bentley. I thought we might have a problem
driving across London, but the police waved us along with their
apparent blessing. On our usual trip to Wales we passed through
Coventry, and this time were impressed by the new and very
modern cathedral that had been built adjacent to the ruins of the
old one, which had been destroyed during the war. A small
wooden cross had been errected on the site. It is made from
burnt timbers and bears the inscription: "Forgive them, they
know not what they do." In Wales, across the Menai Straits
from the house in which we lived for a time during the war, we
visited another church. This was the church of Saint Tvsilio, built
in the year 630. It is one of the oldest churches in Britain.

Back in Redlands, I met Prince Ahmad ibn Saud of Saudi
Arabia. He was a student at the University of Redlands. He
had his Alvis sports car for sale and knowing the reputation of
the make, I was very quick to buy it. I was one of the few people
in the area who knew the value of the car and the prestige it
carried in Europe. Prince Phillip owned one! Bill had a lot of
fun with his antique cars and nearly sold one to Tony Curtis.

1963 was not a traveling year but we were busy again with
our musical life, and in the Redlands Bowl we performed *Turandot, Brigadoon* and *The Mikado* often with audiences of over
5,000.

Achmed returned from Saudi Arabia with his new bride.
She could speak very little English and Megan and some of
the other ladies enjoyed introducing her to the complexities of
American life.

The following year was an important one for the family.
Simine and Bill were married and so the family was enriched
with a member of the royal family of Iran. We naturally became
very interested in that country and what a fascinating historical
background it has. Later in the same year Bill set off on a
world tour. He and Simine spent some time with the shah's
family on holiday on the Caspian coast. This was very interesting
for Bill. He said that Queen Farah Diba was an intelligent and

attractive lady. As usual, we had been busy at the Redlands Bowl all summer and had performed in the *Gondoliers*, Wagner's *Tännhauser*, and Bach's *Requiem*.

Early in 1965 we made another visit to Britain. We had completed the sale of the farm, which was a great relief. I was interested in returning to Africa. In London I had interviews at Rhodesia House, and at the office of the high commissioner of Zambia. I also had an official medical examination at the Ministry of Overseas Development, which was satisfactory. We visited Joan, who was still stationed in England and living in the Quaker village of Jordans, where William Penn, a Quaker, is buried. We attended a service at the meeting house there. We also went to Brighton to meet our old friend, Norman Hall, who had followed me for the FAO to Iraq. We discussed the relative merits of working and living in Rhodesia and Zambia. Norman had done some work in both countries and he advised Rhodesia.

On our return to Redlands we were again in a number of shows, the most interesting of which was a religious musical called *I Am the Way*, with Jerome Hines, the famous Metropolitan bass, in the lead. In fact, he had written the music. Jerome Hines was a devout man and, being six feet four inches in height, was very impressive in the lead role. It was an inspiring experience. He told us that La Forge, the composer of the *Lord's Prayer*, had been asked to write the music but had refused, saying that the job was too much for him. So Jerome took it on. He worked at it for several months but made little progress. He said that he prayed about it a lot and one day he sat at the piano and was inspired to play some beautiful music. He called his wife, also an opera singer, to listen. She started to weep and said, "Jerome, you alone could not have written that."

Later that year, in August, Joan and her family returned from England. Her husband, now a colonel, was in charge of the officers training corps at the University of the South in Sewanee, Tennessee.

11

RHODESIA

Early in 1966 we were on the move again. I had accepted the appointment in Rhodesia as veterinary research officer with the government. Before we left I received a letter from the director of veterinary services saying that owing to the unilateral declaration of independence, the government funds had been cut and the plans for the expansion of the laboratory had been dropped. However, I was now anxious to go. We sold our Spanish style house for $17,000. The interesting point here is that now, ten years later, it is valued at over $40,000.

We were happy that our grandson, John, had just been born and that our links with Iran were stronger than ever. After seeing Simine, Bill, and John in Los Angeles, we flew to Tennessee to to see Joan and her family, then on to New York to see the Kudernas, friends of Auburn days. Strange things happen sometimes and little did we think that in five years time we would meet the Kudernas in London—when I met the queen—and then in Kenya.

We were only in London a few days before leaving for Rhodesia, but we did meet the Pitcairns from Cyprus days. En route we put down in Entebbe, Uganda, and I could just see the laboratory in which I worked forty years before.

On arrival in Salisbury we were met by Holly Thornton, a friend of my student days, in Liverpool, who quickly steered us through the customs and other formalities. Holly was advising the government on meat inspection and had an important position, since meat, in spite of the sanctions, was almost the only Rhodesian export. We soon found accommodation in a residential hotel with our flat in pleasant grounds.

The government supplied me with transportation pending

the arrival of my Alvis car, which had been shipped from Los Angeles. This arrived in Beira Mozambique in about a month. We flew down in a high-winged monoplane; I think it was an old German Fokker. We found our shipping agent but it was some time before we could get the car started. We had a most interesting trip through the typical African countryside of Mozambique. All this was virgin territory to us. It was late when we arrived at Umtali on the Rhodesian border to find that our car papers were not in order. It was a good hour before the customs relented and let us through. In Salisbury the Alvis was a sensation and never ceased to be a focus of attention. The British, like some others, have a "thing" about special cars— and mine was a beauty!

Rhodesia has been very much in the public eye for a number of years and now seems to be faced with the ultimate crisis in the present Geneva Conference. We arrived there soon after the unilateral declaration of independence, and so for three years were in close contact with the important events of that time.

It is necessary to look briefly at the historical background of the country. The Portuguese explorers had penetrated into the country in very early days without leaving much of a lasting impression. David Livingstone reached the Victoria Falls in 1855. The native name of the falls is *Mosioatunya,* which means smoke does sound there. In describing the falls, Livingstone says, in part:

> ... we came in sight for the first time of the columns of vapour appropriately called 'smoke' rising at a distance of five or six miles, exactly as when large tracts of grass are burned in Africa. Five columns now arose, and bending in the direction of the wind, they seemed placed against a low ridge covered wilth trees; the tops of the columns at this distance appeared to mingle with the clouds. They were white below, and higher up became dark, so as to simulate smoke very closely. The whole scene became extremely beautiful; the banks and islands dotted over the river are adorned with sylvan vegetation of great variety and form. At the period of

our visit, several trees were spangled over with blossoms. There, towering over all, stands the great burly baobab, each of whose enormous arms would form the trunk of a large tree, beside a group of graceful palms which, with their feathery-shaped leaves depicted on the sky, lend their beauty to the scene. Creeping with awe to the verge I peered down and saw that the stream 1,000 yards broad leaped down 100 feet and then became compressed into a space of 15 or 20 yards.

Dr. Moffat founded the first permanent settlement at the Inyati Mission in 1859. The pioneer column went north from the Transvaal and founded Fort Salisbury in 1890. The mining of gold was not a great success, but there was good cheap land available. Cecil Rhodes obtained a royal charter in 1889 and founded the British South Africa Company. There was some fighting with Chief Lobenguela, who finally signed away mineral and land rights. There were and are two main tribes in Rhodesia—the Mashona and the Mtabele. The former are the most numerous and peaceful, the latter a more warlike tribe who constantly raided and subdued the Shona.

Dr. Gilfand, a prominent surgeon and a professor of Medicine in Salisbury, for whom I had the pleasure of giving some joint lectures on brucellosis at the medical school, has written a number of books describing the character and social customs of the Shona as the result of an intensive and thorough study carried out after living many years in close contact with them. He considers them to be one of the most peace-loving people in the world. Professor Gilfand said that the morals of the Shona were exemplary. Good morals and behavior are tied up with character. "No man works alone. All are geared to interdependence. There is always a home for members of the family and no one can be removed from his holdings. No one will be deserted in time of need. How can such mores be classed as barbaric? They deserve the highest praise." The Shona chief, as Gilfand knew him, was no despot. Women are certainly polite before men, frequently eating alone, sometimes kneeling before them, but this does not mean that they are treated badly. Each have their duties to perform. The man is not a free agent. For example, he cannot freely dispose of property. It can be seen that the Shona have been a very easy people for the settlers to deal with from the beginning.

For the first thirty-two years Rhodesia was governed by a charter company. In 1922 it voted against union with South Africa, preferring to retain its ties with the United Kingdom. More recently a federation was formed of Southern and Northern Rhodesia and Nyasaland. It seemed to be a viable proposition but it eventually collapsed. Administration and business was concentrated in the South, copper wealth in the North, and agriculture in Nyasaland. Each had advantages but much of the political power was in the South. And so was formed Rhodesia, Zambia, and Malawi.

Garfield Todd became prime minister. He was a farmer and missionary. The key to the political future rested on the franchise. Land apportionment and education were sore points. Todd was sympathetic toward black aspirations. He was replaced by Winston Fields, a sort of compromise, but after a few months Ian Smith, who was very much a Front man, took over the office. It could be seen that much maneuvering had been going on to establish a strong white supremist as prime minister. Meanwhile, in 1964, Sir Douglas Hume, the British prime minister, laid down the principles upon which Britain was prepared to grant independence. They were:

1. Unimpeded progress to majority rule.
2. Immediate improvement in the political status of the African people.
3. Progress to end discrimination.
4. Guarantees against retrogressive legislation.
5. Preparation for independence acceptable to the people as a whole, with no oppression of minority by majority regardless of race.

An election was held in which the Front made it clear that it would not consider a victory a mandate for unilateral declaration of independence. Of course in the end they did. It seemed obvious that Ian Smith and the Front were determined on a unilateral decelaration of independence. Harold Wilson was now prime minister of Britain and became the target for every smear the Rhodesians could think up. Ian Smith rejected a proposal for a meeting with the Commonwealth Ministers. Things were now happening fast. Smith proclaimed a three months state of emergency. Todd was restricted to his farm and Smith rejected the terms of a royal commission. On November 9, he sent a message of loyalty to the queen; on November 11, a unilateral declaration of independence was proclaimed. The governor, Sir Humphrey Gibbs, was a highly respected native Rhodesian who refused to resign. Sanctions were imposed by the United Nations but the United States continued to buy chrome, and other countries still imported Rhodesian meat.

So we arrived in Rhodesia early in 1966 under very strange circumstances. It was thrilling to be back in Africa again. Once visited, it never loses its appeal. The countryside and the climate were beautiful and Salisbury was a most attractive city. There was, however, a tenseness in the air that we did not expect. Many of the whites felt a great bitterness toward Britain, and there was a lot of talk about fighting—but whom to fight? The British prime minister had stated that there would be no military intervention. One had to be careful in conversation not to say anything against the Front. In fact, at tea break in the laboratory about a dozen people would sit around and not say a word. Yes, these times were a bit of a strain.

Soon strict censorship of the newspapers and the radio were imposed. Some days many colums of the paper would be completely blank. A friend of mine who was working as a reporter found it difficult and decided to try the radio. He said that it was worse, with someone standing over you every minute checking every word. Petrol was rationed and there was a bit of belt tightening but not much real hardship to the white citizen.

There was a large Welsh group in Salisbury and one of our very first engagements was to attend the Saint David's Day dinner at Meikles Hotel, where I was asked to toast the visitors. To show how small the world is, it turned out that at the next table sat a lady who went to school with Megan in Llanrwst many years ago.

Before we left Redlands our friend Dr. Hern, who had met a Mr. Christie in the then Northern Rhodesia, told us to get in touch with him, and this we did. We found the Christies to be very interesting people. Mrs. Christie was born in Rhodesia and I believe her mother came up with the pioneers. The former, under the name of Phillipa Beryl, has written several books on the Rhodesian problem, of which she naturally has much knowledge. At our first visit she asked me many questions, obviously interested in the reactions of a newcomer to the scene. Christie was a barrister and, at the time, was on a list of rather undesirables that Smith kept. Later he seemed to shift his ground and became dean of the law department at the university.

About the same time we met another young barrister and his wife. She was a South African and discreetly volunteered the information that her father, who was well over seventy years old, had just been put into prison by the South African government. He was accused of being a Communist. We presumed that his main offense was in being problack. They were an interesting and pleasant couple, and since that time we have noticed that when an important case involving the Rhodesian government and a black is tried, the defending barrister is often our friend.

One of the greatest pleasures Megan and I had in Africa was watching big game. We had many opportunities to do this in Rhodesia and later in Kenya. It was, of course, a nostalgic experience for us. Mana Pools, on the banks of the Zambesi, had a great attraction because here one could get away from motels and camp out and also walk around without being chased by a game warden! It was a little more like the Africa of 1926. Our first visit was after we had been to a conference in Lusaka. One of my colleagues, Fritz Herchemeyer, drove us in his light truck. We stayed with Mr. Colley, a veterinary officer who also flew his own plane. He was getting out of Zambia and he was going to fly out two planes—I think as a way of getting some of his assets out of the country. Fritz and I made some contributions to the conference and had a good time meeting some old friends. On the return journey we camped on the banks of the river. Megan and I slept in the truck and Fritz under a mosquito net. Elephants were snooping around the camp during the night but we kept very quiet and all was well. On the way out of the reserve we ran into a big herd, so we stopped the car and Megan and I climbed down to try to get some pictures. We were behind the truck when some of the elephants, including a large bull, decided to investigate *us!* Fritz started to take off and we had to run for it and scramble on board.

On one trip to Zambia we went with Dexter Chavanduka. This time we went to the veterinary laboratory at Mazabuka, which is about sixty miles out of Lusaka. It was greatly understaffed and I was glad that I had chosen to go to Salisbury. Mrs. Hobday, a British veterinarian, was in charge. She was rather unusual and had a collection of domestic and wild animals, including a gaggle of geese that set up a terrific noise about 5:00 A.M. every day. Major Hobday, her husband, was another of the first of the flying vets. I am afraid that he had flown off to Ethiopia, and I do not think he came back. His uncle was Sir Fred Hobday, a famous British veterinarian in the days of the horse. He was dean of the London Veterinary College. On the return trip it was a bright moonlight night when we settled down at the Mana Pools. Megan and I slept in a pup tent and Dexter slept in the truck. We were sleeping with the open door facing the Zambezi. During the night I heard some splashing, and getting up I saw two elephants swimming toward the riverbank. I woke Megan and Dexter up. Our two visitors changed course and headed for a nearby island. It was a most beautiful sight. Later in the tour we went to Wankie Game Park and were fortunate enough to get close to a herd of the rather rare sable antelope outside of the park. In fact, we were able to get out of the car and make a close approach. Inside the reserve we spent several hours in one of the game-watching stands. We were alone for most of the day, and this, of course, makes the African bush so appealing.

Our next visit to a game reserve was to Gorongosa, in Mozambique. This time we decided to take with us Dexter Chavanduka and his wife. We had a shock when we arrived at Umtali, on the border, to find that none of the cafes would serve us with tea or food because we were with black friends. Then Mrs. Chavanduka found that her passport was not in order. So we went to the Old Umtali Mission and had tea there. Her father was a preacher and had been at the mission for many years. The three of us decided to go on. I thought the atmosphere over the border was easier for Dexter to handle. It was a rough ride through the reserve but very beautiful. The first camp the Portugese had made was subject to floods, and so a new site was found. The old buildings had been taken over by lions. We have some close pictures of lions basking on the porch, and one movie shot of a lion climbing very leisurely up the external stairway. We were riding around one day in the Alvis and met a German boy in a Volkswagon. He had just seen a pride of lion in the tall grass. We could not take our car there, so we got into his and he drove so close that we could have literally touched the animals. One young cub was very angry and made a good picture. Megan and I made another trip later on to Mozambique, this time to Beira where forty years before she had gone ashore and picked up a severe malarial infection. This time it was all sunshine.

Each developing country has its own particular pattern, or environment, within the framework of which a veterinary or other project has to be carried out. With the American AID program in Israel, my work was largely associated with well-trained and experienced personnel in an intensively organized agricultural community with a high proportion of veterinary staff to animal population. In Iraq, on a mission for the Food and Agriculture Organization of the United Nations, I found that at that time a situation consisting of a depleted and somewhat rundown veterinary laboratory service and little technical assistance or equipment was all that was available. In Rhodesia I found a still different situation. At the laboratory the experienced technicians were already fully occupied on diagnostic work, vaccine production, and other duties. In the field the professional and lay staff were at least at the beginning of the survey under strength, with large geographical areas to cover.

In considering what methods to adopt in carrying out a survey, there were obvious differences between the black African and the white or European areas. It should be noted that there is a Land Apportionment Act which separates the two areas. The type of cattle and kind of animal husbandry also are different. The European farmer may have a dairy or beef herd or both types of herd on the same farm. The African's are essentially of the beef type and the husbandry methods less developed. While the tribes are nomadic, the animal husbandry is essentially of the range type.

The object of this study was to determine, if possible, the incidence and distribution of brucellosis in Rhodesia. In fact, the work was principally concerned with contagious abortion in cattle. Historically, the disease is important in this country for it was here in 1927 that Bevan, the then director of veterinary research, suspected that undulant fever in man was contracted from cows infected with contagious abortion. An early interest in this problem thus existed. As early as 1914, Bevan had confirmed the disease serologically in cattle. Mention of the disease was made in every annual report of the director of veterinary services, but no proper attempt was made to determine the size of the problem. In 1966, however, it was thought that the presence of this disease might militate against the export of beef to certain countries, and it was decided to determine the extent of the problem with the view of possible control measures being taken on a national level. Early in the survey, a Departmental Brucellosis Committee was set up, of which I was chairman. A statistical analysis of the results of the survey was not contemplated, and indeed not considered necessary, for our purpose.

The survey was complicated by the fact that at first there appeared to be no satisfactory way to collect blood samples from the African areas. Attempts were made to collect milk samples from individual cows. This method was stopped because of the difficulty of sending the samples long distances without adequate transportation. The problem was solved by taking blood samples from cattle at the dipping centers. The samples were identified as to Tribal Trust Land or Native Purchase Area and Dipping Center. In this way we were able to determine the incidence at each center. The sampling percent of the cow population varied from 4 percent to 10 percent. A very wide geographical area was covered and the sampling percentage was satisfactory. There were significant variations in the incidence of the disease. In Salisbury, the incidence was 0.5 percent, in Umtali 1.8 percent, in Bulawayo 1.7 percent, in Chipinga 3.8 percent, in Fort Victoria 5.1 percent, and in Gwanda Province 5.2 percent. These figures and the fact that we identified the Dipping Centers will have an important bearing on control measures.

As a screening test for brucellosis in cows, the value of the Milk Ring Test (MRT) is well established. The false positive reactions that may occur due to the inclusion of the drying off cow and the difficulty in interpreting tests—due to mastitis or the souring of the milk—should be remembered.

The five main milk collecting depots in Rhodesia are widely separated, so that by checking all the depots geographically the whole country was covered. A large percentage of cream samples arriving in Salisbury were also tested by a modified Ring Test. This work could be extended.

Our aim was to do the M.R.T. every three months, but this soon became impossible; so the time interval in some cases was longer. In spite of this the exercise was very valuable in many ways. The techniques of collecting, dispatching, and testing the samples under local conditions were demonstrated. Most of the infected herds have now been identified and with continued testing this information will be maintained. The approximate herd incidence at the various depots was: Gwelo 13.8 percent, Bulawayo 7.5 percent, Umtali 2.5 percent, Salisbury 11.4 percent, and Gatooma 33 percent. By carrying out serological tests on a number of herds, we have shown that those positive to the M.R.T. invariably contain positive reactors. In the Salisbury area 16 of these herds were tested and reactors were found in each case.

Of 1,512 cows tested, 7.8 percent reacted. On the other hand when 9 herds that had passed three consecutive M.R.T. were tested, very few cows reacted. Of 736 cows, only 1.3 percent reacted. Of the 10 cows that reacted, 5 were from a herd with a history of adult vaccination. The value of the M.R.T. as a screening test and as part of a control program is, I believe, well proven by these results.

Most of the samples of cream received at the Salisbury Milk Depot were tested once. Only 3 out of 303 were positive. In addition, 5 farms retailing milk were tested, and only 1 was positive. A herd test revealed one reactor with a titre of 2,560 i.u. This was an interesting result in view of the owner's statement that this was a self-contained herd.

After some discussion by the Brucellosis Committee, it was decided to determine the incidence in beef herds by taking samples from cows sent for slaughter to the main abattoirs. It was realized that a small number of dairy cows and cull cows would be involved and some from African areas. However, an examination of some positive lots revealed that a great majority of them came from European beef herds. Lot numbers obtained when the samples were collected enabled us to identify the owners.

During an intense period of sampling, which extended over a period of several months, from 40 to 70 percent of cows slaughtered were sampled. This is considered very satisfactory for survey purposes. The total abattoir test results indicated an incidence varying from less than 1 percent to 7.2 percent.

Geographically the variations in incidence were confirmed to a large extent by all methods of survey. In the northern districts, that is in the Umtali, Rusape, and Salisbury areas, the incidence was generally low. In the African cows in much of this area, it was less than 1 percent. There was, however, one pocket of heavy infection in the Sabi Tribal Trust Land. The incidence in the European beef cattle in the above districts was 3.2 percent, except that in the Umtali area it appeared to be less than 1 percent. The kill at this center was small. In the southern part of the country the incidence in African cows and European beef cows was higher.

In African cows it was approximately 5 percent with some pockets of still heavier infection. In the beef cows the incidence at Fort Victoria abattoir was 7.2 percent and Bulawayo 5.8 percent.

In the screening tests of the licensed dairy herds, it was again seen that the incidence in the Umtali area was low, being only 2.2 percent. The herds servicing the Gatooma Depot appeared to be heavily infected, the incidence being approximately 33 percent. Little herd testing had been done in this district, but it appeared from reports received that the positive reactions were essentially due to infection and not to adult vaccination. The incidence in Bulawayo appears to have dropped from 13.2 percent to 7.5 percent during the testing period. In Salisbury and Cwelo, the herd incidence remained about the same during the testing period, namely 11 percent in the former and 13.8 percent in the latter.

The overall incidence in the dairy herds was 12 percent. Infected dairy herds tested revealed an incidence in the Salisbury area of 7.3 percent and in Bulawayo of 18 percent.

The most important finding of the side investigations was the isolation of Br.suis from a goat, this being the first time the organism had been recognized in Rhodesia. This is the species of brucella that is most pathogenic to man and that infected our guinea pig colony. This resulted in the accidental infection of a number of the laboratory assistants, some of whom were hospitalized. Fortunately, they all recovered. I was overseas on leave at the time. However, because I had originally isolated the organism, I will long be remembered in the laboratory!

A number of meetings were held by the Departmental Brucellosis Committee, and all aspects of control measures that might be introduced were considered. However, apparently owing to the shortage of staff and funds, at this time extensive measures of control and eradication were not envisaged.

In spite of these seeming difficulties, I presently believe that it is very important that some attempt be made to tackle the problem—no matter how limited the scale. The activities connected with the survey program have stimulated an interest in the disease, and the introduction of some control measures would, I believe, find a satisfactory degree of support from most of the farming community.

My recommendations were compiled in an official report, the basic substance of which is as follows: It is my strong feeling that we have an efficient and economical method available for locating infected herds and similarly a means of determining clean herds. As a first step in control, I suggest the formation of a register of clean dairy herds. I feel that it is time the Rhodesian veterinary department took upon itself this responsibility. All dairy herds that have passed three consecutive Milk Ring Tests should be blood tested. Reactors should be branded with a view to early elimination from the herd and, finally, to the admission of the herd to the clean register. Retention on the register would be subject to continued negative MRT and any blood tests deemed necessary by the department. Failure to pass any test would result in suspension of the herd from the register, pending subsequent satisfactory tests. Regulations covering movement of cattle into these herds would be required. In fact, some control on the movement of cattle from known infected herds is very urgently needed. All other dairy herds should be blood tested as soon as possible and the reactors branded. This should include herds that supply cream.

In known infected areas, both European and African, I would suggest the immediate official inoculation of calves with Strain 19. Where necessary, the use of killed vaccine for adult cows is advocated. In areas where the incidence is very low, say less than 1 percent, some consideration should be given to a plan of herd testing and the removal of reactors. The survey should be extended to include the other important species, such as goat, sheep, and the pig.

The former director, Mr. T. Lees May, the present director, Mr. J. M. Williams, and Mr. G. Christie, the director of the laboratory, were all very cooperative and the report was very well received. Apart from the survey I was for six months in charge of rabies diagnosis, a very important job at a time when the disease was spreading rapidly, especially in jackals. For a time it was a threat to the city of Salisbury. We were using the then new Fluorescent Antibody Test and confirming it by mouse inoculation. I had seen the former technique in California, where I was assured of its complete efficacy. It is, of course, much quicker than the mouse test, which might take as long as three weeks. Also the mouse test requires much more care, since one may be handling highly infective material and a syringe at the same time.

12

IRAN

Simine and Bill were in Iran for the coronation of the Shah, and they invited us to go over. We were very excited with the idea. We found that owing to the mysteries concerning air miles we could fly via London for less money than the direct flight. I have never been able to work that one out! So we went via Luanda and Lisbon and then on to England. We saw Joan and her family again in Jordan before we left for Rome and Tehran. We arrived late at night and were duly impressed by being met by a chauffeur with one of the royal cars. We went for a very late supper to the house of Amer—one of Simine's brothers. Simine had another brother, Cyrus. Both brothers studied in Germany while Simine found her way to the United States after attending school in Egypt.

This was the first of many visits to Tehran. Recently we had the honor of being received as dinner guests by Princess Shams—the elder sister of the shah.

We stayed for a while in a cottage in the grounds of Princess Aschraf's house, situated at the foot of Mount Damavand, which is 9,000 feet high and usually has some snow on the summit. The establishment was quite impressive with royal guards at the gates, and no one was permitted in or out without being scrutinized. It was a very different life-style. Simine and Bill had many precoronation engagements, including dinner at the prime minister's, Mr. Hovedas, and so on. We enjoyed keeping an eye on young John. We were not sure if we ourselves would be invited to the coronation, so with Bill we flew to Ishfahan and Shiras. The former has the great square or Midan, where several hundred years ago the shah of the time played polo. It is now a miniature lake. Around it are beautiful mosques and palaces. Some

of the former are of indescribable beauty, with their dramatic
form and glazed tile covering. There is also a famous hotel there—
the Shah Abbas. It presents a scene of beauty out of the *Arabian
Nights.*

Shiraz is situated at a height of 5,000 feet, and the climate
is pleasant, tropical, and stimulating. It was the home of two of
Persia's greatest poets—Hafis and Saadi. Hafis never left the
city. Saadi wandered over the known world. From Shiraz we had
the wonderful experience of visiting the famous ruins of Persepolis, which were built by Darius and were the pride of Persia
2,500 years ago. Part of an inscription on the tomb of Darius
located some miles from Persepolis reads, "A great god is
Ahmamazda who created the earth, who created yonder sky,
who made Darius King, who created man, who created happiness
for man." Cyrus, who was one of the rulers then, is of course
mentioned in the Old Testament.

Waiting for us on our return to Tehran was an invitation to
the coronation, though not actually inside the palace, which was
reserved almost entirely for the family, but in the grounds where
stands had been erected. We had a rush to get proper clothing;
we both needed full-evening dress. Megan, of course, had to have
hers made, and after some problems a beautiful job was done. I
found mine in the back room of a Jewish carpet seller! We appeared in our places at 10:00 A.M. It was a wonderful, colorful
occasion. The red carpet came very close to where we were sitting, and we had a splendid view of the shah, the queen, and the
young prince as they walked with great dignity to their waiting
carriages. Later we saw Simine and Bill waving from one of the
palace windows. Coming back to town on the bus we spoke to
a couple sitting near us who were in ordinary clothes. The man
said he was a Harley Street specialist visiting the university and
had been invited to attend the ceremony.

Soon Simine and Bill made a trip to the Caspian in one of
the royal planes. Our liberal-minded son was certainly getting
around.

Before we left Iran, Simine took us to the old palace of her
grandfather, the founder of the regime. It is now a private

museum and contains one of the oldest and largest Persian rugs in existence.

It was now time to say good-bye and we left Iran after one of the most interesting experiences of our lives. We arrived in Jerusalem in the evening and went immediately to Saint Georges Hostel. This, we thought, was an ideal place to stay; though without the luxury of the large hotels, it was more in keeping with the historical background of the city. We loved seeing once again the famous old sites, including the Tomb in the Garden. In Jaffa we stayed with the Allisons at the Anglican Mission. We called at the embassy and after many years were recognized by some of the staff. It is nice to be remembered. Apart from an eight-hours wait in Johannesburg, our flight to Salisbury was uneventful.

We plunged immediately into our busy life. Megan was busy with the Cambrian Society. I had been made one of the veterinarians at the racetrack, and this kept me busy on weekends. One day Ian Smith, the prime minister, came along with me to the starting gate. Politics was not the topic of conversation. Part of my duty at the track was to carry out the dope test when requested, but during the two years I was officiating, there was little trouble.

We were very active in the Salisbury chorus and did a number of performances in the attractive cathedral. One evening the Reverend Granville Morgan from the Presbyterian church and Dean Sam Wood from the cathedral came in for dinner. We found that they came from the same small village in South Wales. Granville was a great orator in the Welsh tradition, while Sam was concerned with the meticulous performances of the sacraments. It was an interesting development in two men from the same small mining village.

We had a slight introduction to the Irish problem from the Meekins and the Stewarts, both from Northern Ireland. Meekin was an ex-R.A.F. officer full of blarney, and both men were somewhat interested in the occult. Stewart was the pig expert. They took very strong and I thought very narrow views of Christianity and Protestantism.

Of the Rhodesian blacks, the Chavandukas were the best known to us. Dexter was the veterinarian and Gordon was a university lecturer and is now the secretary to the Reverend Mr. Maserowa—leader of perhaps the strongest Rhodesian party. One evening we invited some friends, including Dexter and Gordon, to dinner. It could not be served in the hotel dining room because of our black friends, but we could have sandwiches served in our cottage on the hotel grounds.

Sir Henry Gibbs was then trying to stick it out as governor, but of course he was not recognized by the rebel government. Before he finally left Government House, we had the pleasure of meeting him at a reception there.

We made two other trips out of the country, one to Beira on the Mozambique coast, where Megan first landed in 1927; the other was to Gaberones, the capital of Botswana. The president there was married to an Englishwoman, the daughter of the late Sir Stafford Cripps, a socialist leader. On a trip into the countryside, we arrived in a village when there was a dance in progress. We joined in the fun. The Africans here, although seemingly poorer than those in Rhodesia, seemed happier. Perhaps it is not only riches that bring happiness.

In Salisbury we visited the Dombashawa caves to see the cave drawings, suggesting that here, hundreds of years ago, man had developed some kind of artistic ability.

Until we left the country late in 1969, there were many meetings between British ministers and the Smith government, all to no avail; now ten years after the unilateral declaration of independence, Smith is at Geneva with his back to the wall and is facing the threat of serious racial conflict in Southern Africa. A pity that statesmanship, rather than politics, could not have prevailed from the beginning.

We loved Rhodesia but in October we had to bid a sad farewell to our friends in Salisbury. Dexter Chavanduka was one in a large group seeing us off at the airport.

Once again we spent a few days in Rome before proceeding to Britain and, almost immediately after, to the States—this time to Sewanee. There is nothing in Sewanee except the University of the South and a very small village. Fortunately for us there is also a small hospital. Megan had been sick in Rhodesia and a number of X-rays had been taken, but the problem had been missed. A crisis occurred and we just managed to get Megan to the hospital. A young surgeon, Dr. Parsons, looked at the X-rays again and detected the trouble. He operated and undoubtedly saved Megan's life. We can never be grateful enough for the kindness and attention given to Megan by the staff and some of the townspeople whom we had met. Joan was at hand, of course, and Bill flew in from Los Angeles. Sad to say that Dr. Parsons was killed a few months later when thrown from his horse.

When Megan was sufficiently recovered, we drove across the country in five days. Megan stood up to the journey well. Bill and his family were in Los Angeles and we spent a pleasant Christmas with them.

When in London I had called at the headquarters of the Voluntary Service Overseas concerning an assignment. This is an organization comparable to the Peace Corps, but not so well financed or so generous in their allowances. I soon received a letter from the VSO offering me an appointment in Kabete, Kenya, as lecturer at the Animal Health and Training Institute. We were delighted to have the opportunity of returning to Africa.

Members of the State University of New York technical advisory group with then New York Governor Averell·Harriman (fourth from left). In 1955 I joined the SUNY group, which aided the American Overseas Mission in Israel.

Our milkman in Ramat Gan, a suburb of Tel Aviv. We were fortunate in finding a furnished house in Ramat Gan; in fact, we lived directly across the street from the American ambassador to Israel.

When I accepted an appointment as veterina
officer in Rhodesia in 1966, the country was the
as it is now, very much in the public eye. Lef
Rhodesia School for the Blind. Center: Meg
with our good friend Dexter Chavanduka, standi
right, in the Native Purchase Area. Top: Ma
Pools Camp, where Megan and I observed l
game on the banks of the Zambesi River.

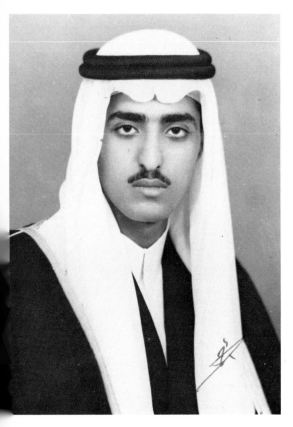

Prince Ahmad ibn Saud of Saudi Arabia. I met the prince when he was a student at the University of Redlands, California. I'll forever be grateful to the prince for selling me his Alvis sports car. Above: The Alvis in front of the Veterinary Research Laboratory in Salisbury, Rhodesia. Left: Megan and I, with the Alvis, in Mozambique.

The Cradle of Western Civilization. Above:
*Megan and Bill in front of the Sacred Bull of
Persepolis, in present-day Iran. Left: Megan and
I at the Sacred Bull of Nimrud in the ruins of
Nineveh, many years before our visit to
Persepolis. We visited Nineveh—the great
Assyrian capital—during my service in Iraq.*

*The coronation of Mohammad Reza
Shah Pahlavi. Our ties with Iran
go beyond the usual tourist sort—
our son's wife, Simine, is the shah's
niece. Simine and Bill were married
in 1964.*

His Imperial Majesty, Reza Shah Pahlavi, father to the present shah of Iran.

Simine, left, and Princess Aschraf, the shah's twin sister, with Nikita Khruschev in Moscow, 1964.

*Scenes from Kenya, where
I lectured at the Animal
Health and Industry Training
Institute.* Above: Baobab
tree in the Tsavo Game
Reserve. Right: Masai
*woman demanding from me
a fee for her photograph.*

Left: *A lion marks his territory
in the Nairobi Game Park.* Below: *Dancing Masai and Megan.*

Above: *A Masai maiden. The girl in profile, whom we met in Nairobi, is wearing her hair in the distinctive Kikiyu style.*

In Nairobi, Megan and I had the pleasure of meeting His Royal Highness Prince Charles and Her Royal Highness Princess Anne.

Two great moments in my life. My daughter, Joan, and Megan with me in front of Buckingham Palace, where I was invested as a Member of the Civil Division of the Most Excellent Order of the British Empire, 1972. My grandson John Manouchehr behind the wheel of a 1934 Lagonda—already showing that Manley penchant for adventure and travel!

13

KENYA

In London we were briefed at the VSO office and were given another medical. Now we found that we could not leave for at least two weeks, so we decided to spend the time at Brighton on the South Coast. It was cheaper than staying in London—as a volunteer, my finances had to be considered. We went on the bus, which was a fairly new experience for us and a pleasant one. Ann Sloan, daughter of our journalist friend in Rhodesia, came over to see us. Soon we had our flying orders and left London on a BOAC plane on April 11. The British Council takes care of volunteers overseas, and Mr. Bird of the Nairobi office met us. Dr. Mann, the project director for the Food and Agricultural Organization at the Animal Health and Training Institute (where I was going to teach), took us to lunch at his house. He has perhaps the most important private collection of Africana in existence. This was my first meeting with this remarkable man, whom I was to know well during the next three and a half years. He was a dynamic and sometimes difficult man, but we got along well. Apart from his work at AHITI, he became world famous for his research on schistosomaisis. The school was not in session but Megan and I went there to a National Food Congress and Freedom from Hunger meeting. Later we were made members of one of the organizing committees. There were always meetings of this kind going on at AHITI.

After a few days we moved into a residential hotel called the Safarilands, owned by M. Sheik—a member of a wealthy Sikh family. We had our own cottage and used the communal dining room. We stayed there on several occasions for extended periods. It was a great place to meet people from all over the world. We bought an English Ford and so became mobile. At the Christian Science church we met Lady Elizabeth Erskine, whose husband had been a member of the Legislative Council and a supporter of President Mzee Jomo Kenyatta.

This might be a good time to look briefly at the history of Kenya. Basically the people of the area are Bantu but with a strong North Kenyan infiltration of slight physique and fine features—resembling more the Ethiopians or Egyptians. The Arabs were the first non-Africans to settle along the East Coast. They penetrated inland only in search of slaves and ivory. They were followed by the Portugese. Prior to 1880 there had been some little exploration inland, mainly by missionaries and others such as Speke, Burton, Thomson, Bishop Hannington, and some Germans. Some of their experiences make for fascinating reading. I have some books published at that time, which reveal how little was known about Africa south of the Sahara.

Life was very primitive for the natives, although they had their unwritten laws and codes. The amenities of so-called civilization were absent. The nomadic tribes lived from their cattle, sheep, and goats. The settled tribes cultivated the land—corn, potatoes, millet, bananas, and other fruit. The land was beautiful and the climate in the Highlands well-nigh perfect, but not so in other parts of the country. Unfortunately, malaria, sleeping sickness, and other diseases were prevalent, and health statistics were not good. The most important early development was the construction of the railway from the coast through to Uganda. This followed the Berlin Conference of 1884 and the rough allocation of the land between Britain and Germany, the former claiming Kenya and Uganda, and the latter Tanganyika. The British East Africa Company was given power to develop the land. Missionaries, soldiers, and some settlers came in, but the company soon found that the charter was not a profitable undertaking; then the British government took over. At one time the construction of the railway was made difficult by the man-eating lions of Tsavo. Many of the laborers on the line were Indians who later set up their dukas or little shops in the villages.

They were prepared to rough it and many of them did well. There is no doubt that some of them took advantage of the natives and became unpopular, but perhaps this is a facet of all trading.

There are some interesting stories about early settlers. The country was very sparsely settled by the indigenous population. There was not a harbor except those for dhows and canoes. There were no roads and outside the Arab coastal area not a stone building, not a school, hospital, or shop. Outside the villages there was a fantastic array of wildlife, man, and cattle.

The old slave routes passed through Kikuyu, where we recently spent two months, and near here the Scottish Mission Hospital was founded in 1890. In 1893, a missionary, the Reverend S. Watt, with his wife and five children, walked from Mombasa to Fort Smith near Kabete—a distance of 300 miles! His youngest child was three months old. The site for the C.M.S. mission was chosen by the Reverend W. A. McGregor in 1901. A mud and straw thatch hut was erected. The famous Leakey family came there in 1902. Mrs. Leakey first came to Kenya in 1892. Canon Leakey immediately started work on the translation of the Bible into Kikuyu. There were three grandsons: one is curator of the Nairobi museum; one carries on the archaeological work of the famous father; and the other has a snake farm out in the bush near Lake Baringo.

Fort Smith is now a private house. There one may look across peaceful countryside to the Veterinary College of the University of Nairobi. There is a small graveyard nearby where a veterinary officer lies buried, killed by the Kikuyu at the turn of the century. Megan and I visited the area several times and, finally one evening after scrambling through bush for a good half-mile, found some gravesites. After removing the grass and branches, we could decipher two of the inscriptions. One read:

> Capt. A. J. Haslam, B.A., M.D., F.R.C.V.S.
> Army Veterinary Dept.,
> Killed by Wakikuyu 23 July 1898.

The other read:

William Alfred Harrison
Died Oct. 1898
From wounds inflicted by a lioness.

Both memorials were erected by friends on the staff of the Uganda railway.

Ewart Grogan came to Africa in 1896. He was a volunteer in a force sent from the south to quell a rising of the Matabele. Previously, he proposed to a young lady but the father-in-law refused consent on the grounds that Grogan had done nothing. Grogan proved him wrong and walked from the Cape to Cairo, which he reached in 1900. With his wife he settled in Kenya in 1904. At that time there were about 600 whites in the country, some sent by their fathers with a hundred pounds or so in their pockets with instructions to make good. Others came to Kenya from patriotic motives, while still others came to make a quick fortune. Land rents were from a half-penny to a penny an acre with an option to buy if the land was improved. Gertrude, Grogan's wife, went to England to have her first baby. On her return Grogan began to build a stone house—one of the first in Nairobi. It was called Chirom. It is now used as a research library. Grogan became a prominent and controversial figure in colonial Kenya and the senior member of the Legislative Council. E. W. Mathis, then sole African representative, said, "My friend Col. Grogan is going to leave behind him when the time comes a tremendous heritage for the future of all races in this country." His wife did a great work for the welfare of the children and on her death Grogan built a children's hospital in her memory. It is there today.

At first the country was run by a small nominated council, and this became a legislative council with a purely white electorate. White settlement was mainly in the Highlands, which was found to be rich agricultural land suitable for raising cattle, sheep, cotton, tea, coffee, and other products. The land was taken from the Masai, Kikuyu, Nandi, and Kipsigis. In the early 1940s, African nationalism was being fostered in Europe by African students, but only in London was it encouraged. On one of the committees was Jomo Kenyatta—a student of anthropology—and a Somali called Mohammed Said. In 1944, Eluid Mathu, a Kikuyu graduate of Balliol College, Oxford, was appointed the first African member of the Legislative Council. He was better educated than most of his European colleagues and so not too popular. The African representation gradually increased. In 1950 Kenyatta returned from Europe and was accused of being involved in the Mau Mau disturbances. He was restricted to a farm in a remote part of the country. During the troubles—mainly between white and Kikuyu and Kikuyu against Kikuyu—the reactions of all parties were atrocious and some of them unbelievable—basically no worse than dropping atomic bombs. In 1958, Mina Amalimba became the first African cabinet minister. Tom Mboya a Luo formed the Convention Peoples Party. Later he became general secretary of the Kenya Federation of Labor, then leader of the Kenya African National Union, and, after independence, minister of economic affairs. In July, 1969, he was shot and killed by an unidentified assassin. Kenyatta was the first prime minister and then president. The road to independence had been cleared by the "Wind of Change" speech made by Prime Minister Macmillan. Many white farmers left the country and the land was taken over by Africans. Many Asians too have been forced to leave. However, quite a number of whites and Asians, especially those born in Kenya, have taken up citizenship. Mzee Jomo Kenyatta has become the grand old man. He has tried to unify the country and up to now has succeeded. He has been prepared to take help from any country—usually without any strings attached.

Because of our romantic association with the country, just being there and traveling around was a continuous thrill for us. For example, on our many trips to Mombasa by road, rarely did we make the 300-mile trip without getting close to elephants and often being chased. Once when we stopped the car, elephants were standing just across the road.

But wildlife was not the only thing at which to marvel. There was the single-track railway, the famous Kenya-Uganda line, and tearing along the road were racing cars taking part in the East African road race, while just up above flew a small plane. Could *this* be the African scene?

In Mombasa we enjoyed walking through the Arab part of the town and visiting the old Portugese fort. Arab dhows have been coming down the coast from the Persian Gulf for centuries. In former days they carried slaves and ivory back. Once Megan and I clambered up the rope to board one of these vessels. It was from Iran, so we had a little in common with the captain. It will be a pity if these picturesque vessels disappear. Once again on the docks we met an American couple traveling around the world on a freighter. There were only six passengers on the ship. And we always visited the cathedral where we were married in 1927. The climate on the coast is, of course, very different from that in Nairobi. The former has the characteristics of the Indian Ocean—warm, humid, with beautiful beaches and waving palm trees. Driving up to Nairobi, 5,000 feet high, in a few hours makes a noticeable change. One of the beautiful sites from the road is the snow-capped summit of Kilimanjaro. This mountain is just over the border of Tanzania. There are no towns of any size along this road. Perhaps this is another of its attractions.

Most people have heard of the famous game reserve near Nairobi. We had yearly tickets so that any day you felt like it you could jump in the car and be in the middle of the reserve in a few minutes. You are not really allowed to get out of your car, but even so it is pleasant just to sit and watch. There are no elephants in this park but most of the other big game and a great variety of birds. Near the main gate is an animal orphanage. We were friends of the warden and came to know some of the orphans well. One side of the reserve is open country, but is so vast that it presents no problem. The game rarely come into town! One day, when the Kudernas were visiting us, we took them out to the reserve in a small Fiat. In a gully we came across a pride of eight lions. We had settled down quite close to them and then found that the car would not start. The game warden happened by in his Land Rover. What to do? He said, "You will have to stay there until the lions move." Just before dusk the pride decided to move off, presumably to start their evening hunt. They moved off slowly one by one—the male being the last to go after deciding to do his business a few yards from the car. Then the warden pulled us out of trouble.

Another evening when on the road from Mombasa, Megan and I entered at one of the smaller reserve gates. We asked the askari on duty if there were any lions in the vicinity. He said, "None anywhere near today, bwana." We had traveled about 100 yards when we saw seven lions approaching down the track! I stopped the car and we just sat still, *very still,* with the windows shut of course. They came straight toward us and passed close along the sides of the car without paying us any attention.

Tsavo is the biggest game reserve in the world, being 8,000 square miles in area. In Tsavo East, marauding lions challenged the first European explorers and the builders of the railway. With Tsavo West, the area forms great elephant country, where upwards of 20,000 elephants and all the species of large mammals and predators live. Here also is Mzima Springs—a beautiful oasislike spot. In fact, the springs supply Mombasa with water. Nearby are pools in which there are hippos and hundreds of fish. In this area you can get out of the car if you are not afraid of monkeys. Once in Tsavo we spent the night in camp on the shores of a small lake. There were no other humans anywhere, and one could enjoy to the full the beauty and the night sounds of the African bush.

We also visited Amboseli Reserve, which is on the Tanzania border and close to Kilimanjaro. We managed to get very close to a cheetah, which is not easy.

The variety of bird life in Kenya is incredible. One week in Nairobi we had a Canadian couple staying with us. The lady was a bird-watcher, and she counted thirty different species in our garden.

Before we finished our tour we made a final visit to Tsavo to once again photograph our elephant friends. We were lucky. We found a small herd watering in a gully. I was able to get out of the car and crawl to the edge, and from about twenty yards I got my pictures. Before leaving elephant country, one must not forget to mention the tree that is so much associated with the terrain. The baobab tree is unique. Elephants love them. They contain much moisture in the enormous trunk. In dry weather when there is a shortage of water, the elephants erode the bark and eat the soft pulp. Unfortunately, the tree is destroyed and since they are slow growing in some areas, they are threatened. It is a fantastic looking tree and when not covered with leaves looks as if it is upside down with the roots in the air. Cream of tartar is obtained from it. Paper, cloth, and rope are made from the bark and the large fruit forms an edible gourd.

The founding of the Animal Health and Industry Training Institute, where I taught, was due to the cooperation of the Kenya government, the U.N. Development Fund, and the Food and Agricultural Organization of the U.N. The history of the institute is a good example of international cooperation for the benefit of a developing nation—and ultimately for us all. The white staff were recruited from the United Kingdom, Holland, France, Germany, and the U.S.A. We were working with African counterparts. Kabete, the town in which AHITI is located, is seven miles from Nairobi and is near the central veterinary research laboratories and the Veterinary School of the University of Kenya. Not far away at Limuru is the East African Agricultural and Veterinary Research Center.

At the institute, I was to teach Microbiology and Preventive Medicine. Shortly after my arrival the students went on strike. I hoped that there was no connection between the two events! The problem was mainly something to do with catering. Anyhow, the students refused to attend classes. It was near the end of term and so after a day of discussion it was decided to close the school until after the vacation. The next term opened on schedule and there was no further trouble. I myself found the students most cooperative.

In describing AHITI, I cannot do better than quote freely from the address of Dr. Mann, the project leader, given at his farewell graduation ceremony: "Some 9 years ago on the site of the institute, goats were grazing. The plan of operation was signed on July 2, 1965, and His Excellency Jomo Kenyatta opened the institute on April 19, 1966. During the next 7½ years, 2,859 students have been enrolled, 263 of whom were foreign students from 18 different countries, including Botswana, Ethiopia, Ghana, Lesotho, Liberia, Malawi, Nigeria, Rhodesia, Rhuanda, South Africa, Southwest Africa, Sudan, Swaziland, Tanzania, Uganda, the West Cameroons, Zambia, and the Seychelles. During the last year, 60 foreign students attended full-time courses. Students in the field are making a valuable contribution to the agricultural economy of the country. Animal health assistants are taking part in the second phase of veterinary activities in Africa. The first was to combat the decimating diseases such as rinderpest, East Coast fever, pleuro-pneumonia, and trypanoso-maisis. The second is to help the farmers to rise from a subsistence to a market economy by adopting modern principles of farming, animal husbandry, artificial insemination, and so on. The institute's graduates have been trained to deal with these new problems. They have served the country well. Two further achievements are announced. Thanks to the generosity of the Swedish people, our education will soon be extended to women; and students from South Sudan are graduating to join those who already returned to serve their home countries in building the nation.

"Because of multi- and bilateral aid, the influx of foreign students, and tutors of many different nationalities, AHITI has become a miniature United Nations Organization where the spirit of understanding, mutual cooperation, tolerance of religion, tribe, color, and race have melted down in one paramount objective—to teach, learn, and apply the acquired knowledge."

Canada, Switzerland, and New Zealand—although they did not contribute to the teaching staff—were among the donor countries, and there have been nongovernmental agencies such as the Rockefeller Foundation and the All Africa Council of Churches that have helped.

Perhaps our closest friends in Kenya were the Logies from Regina, Canada. Hugh was one of the Canadian aid team concerned mainly with raising the standard of education of African teachers. Prior to this time, largely owing to the extreme shortage of teachers, people were employed whose educational standard was slightly lower than that usually required. I think some of my Canadian friends blamed the British for this. It was more difficult than one might think. Suppose in the beginning you have two million illiterate Africans to educate. Where do you get the teachers and the money to do the job? There was no simple solution, and in the very early days, of which the Canadians had very little knowledge, missionaries took the leading part. Another Canadian family was George and Noreen Porozni and their four school-age sons. They had previously been in Nigeria. At one of their parties we met Michaela Dennis—the author of *A Leopard in My Lap*. We met Michaela a number of times, sometimes at her home in Karen on the edge of the game reserve. She was from England and, while working as a model in New York, met Armand Dennis—a movie photographer. They fell in love and found that they had a mutual desire for travel and adventure in remote places. Taking pictures in East Africa for the film *King Solomon's Mines,* they realized that Kenya was to be their home. Armand passed on a few years later, but Michaela kept on the house in Karen where she could be near her beloved animals. She had developed a philosophy—respect for all life—that draws forth love and kindness from all normal men and women. She had no fear of animals. She says, "I have slept with a snake without knowing it and no harm has come to me, but if I had been conscious of its presence and shown resentment and fear, this might have been a different story." At her house she held spiritual healing meetings.

Igor Mann, my immediate superior, rarely spoke of his early days, but apparently he was a refugee from Eastern Europe. He joined the veterinary service and soon became head of the meat hygiene department—an important position in a cattle country such as Kenya. As is shown elsewhere, he took a broad view of his duties as project manager at AHITI and made it of international importance. His wife, Erica, was an architect with the government. One of their daughters working in Germany met an Anglo-German, and they were married in Nairobi. The wedding had the "Mannish" touch. After the wedding by one of the legal officers of the government, we all went out to a Masai village, where the couple were made members of the tribe. The groom was a very tall man, and when the chief fitted him out with a headdress of buffalo horns, he was a very impressive figure.

At Lady Elizabeth's we met a pleasant young man, the son of the late kabaka of Uganda. He was in school in Kenya. Dr. and Mrs. Cooper were close friends. John had been with the Voluntary Service Overseas in Tanzania. He was a specialist in the diseases of snakes and birds. Thanks to John we again met Dr. Leakey. Megan and I had a long session with Dr. Leakey in Limuru, where he had a large colony of chimps. He was studying animal behavior. John is now with the Medical Research Council in London.

Sir William and Lady Duffus, in whose house we lived for several months, were from Jamaica. Sir William was chief justice for the three countries of East Africa. His brother was chief justice of Jamaica and their father was a leading legal light in that country. The son of Sir William and Lady Duffus had qualified as a veterinarian at my old school at Liverpool University and later worked at the research laboratories in Kabete.

We were always invited to functions given by British High Commissioner Sir William Norris and later Sir Anthony Duff. We were fortunate in meeting Prince Charles and his sister Princess Anne on two occasions when they were visiting Kenya. Once we had pleasant conversation with the royal couple and found the prince a very interesting and charming person. Finding out that I was a VSO, he said that, while on safari near Lake Rudolf, he heard of a volunteer who against orders went into the lake for a swim. The lake was infested with crocodiles and the young man had a severe bite on the bottom. He was lucky to escape.

On two occasions Mrs. Orr, a friend from California, brought out groups of tourists to Kenya and I was invited to talk to them about the country. Part of the tour service!

One dance that Megan and I always enjoyed was when we were asked to open the student dance at AHITI. Africans love to dance and they put on quite a show.

In July, 1971, I had completed my assignment, but Dr. Mann was anxious for me to remain for another year. I was very willing but only if I could take some leave in England and the U.S.A. So we left Kenya not being quite sure that we would return.

I had ordered a Peugeot car and went over to Paris to pick it up. We were in something of a hurry to get to Wales in time for the national eisteddfod being held in Bangor. We arrived in a small village late one night and found that the gears of the car were slipping. There was no Peugeot agent within 100 miles. Across the road from the farmhouse where we were staying was a machine shop. It had been a woolen factory—which are still fairly common in rural Wales. There of all places I found a man who was clever enough to get at the gears and weld the broken part. The eisteddfod is an annual musical and cultural festival. It was attended by 20,000 people each day. One period is given to welcoming Welsh visitors from all over the world. It is a nostalgic time and appears on Welsh T.V. The Pullens from Rhodesia were there.

Simine and young John were now in Paris, so we made a trip back crossing on a Hovercraft for the first time. It is quicker—that is about all one can say about it. Simine was staying in a villa belonging to her aunt, Princess Ashraf. We returned quickly to the U.S.A. Bill and a number of senior engineers had been axed. They were working in Atlantic City but did not like the political atmosphere. After the Peugeot arrived we drove across country to Joan's place in Riverside. Her husband was in the Strategic Air Command at Marsh Air Base. After some uncertain moments, we decided to return to Kenya. This time we flew from London to Nairobi on United Arab Airlines with a stop in Cairo. We were able to see the Pyramids for the first time.

We were happy to be back in Nairobi. The Logies were back after a trip to Cyprus to see their son, who was doing voluntary work in a Turkish village.

In November I received a letter from the British high commissioner. I thought at first that it was an invitation to a party, but it was to inform me that my name was being forwarded to Her Majesty the Queen recommending me for a civilian honor. Later I received the following from Sir Eric:

Dear Dr. Manley,

The Queen has been pleased to approve your appointment as a Member of the Civil Division of the Most Excellent Order of the British Empire and that this appointment will be published in the New Year's Honours List, 1972.

I am well aware of the regard you and your work are held in Kabete, and that your contribution in a crucial area of the country's development will be of much value. In addition an award to the Mzee of the VSO programme in Kenya will be of much encouragement to many and I am sure it will give great pleasure and satisfaction to your friends and colleagues as it does to me.

My wife joins me in sending you and your wife our congratulations and warm wishes for the future.

Yours Sincerely,
Eric Norris.

When I received this letter it was the biggest surprise of my life, since I had never given the subject a thought. I felt very honored, and when I went home to tell Megan the pleasure was doubled. We had something of great interest to look forward to—a visit to Buckingham Palace to be received by Her Majesty the Queen. My name was duly included in the New Year's Honours List, 1972. I decided to attend the investiture to be held the following November. Many congratulations were received. I enjoyed them all! My profession was pleased and letters came from the Royal College of Veterinary Surgeons, Liverpool University, and the Royal Commonwealth Society.

Bill had gone to Iran to take up an appointment with the Ministry of Economics. Later he invited us to Iran so we made our second visit there. En route we went again to Israel and stayed at the Saint Georges Hostel. Our old friend the Reverend Roger Allison had been transferred from Jaffa to Jerusalem and he took us around some of the more unusual sites. After a few days we continued our journey to Tehran where we arrived at 4:00 A.M. Bill was there to meet us. This time we saw a lot of Simine's brother, Prince Cyrus, who seemed to spend most of his time writing poetry—perhaps part of his Persian heritage. We met Princess Aschraf again and had a good time with my grandson John. We flew to London on an Aeroflot Jet with a stopover in Moscow. We had no visas so were restricted to the hotel—to one floor in fact! However, we were eventually taken on a guided tour and were duly impressed by the cleanliness and orderliness of the city.

In England we went to the annual veterinary conference at Exeter. Megan noted: "A very pleasant dinner and dance, Mrs. B. fell for Frank—fun!" We were staying at a small, friendly guesthouse. A strange incident happened one day. I went to a soccer match with the son of the house. The referee died on the field. We visited my nephew who was farming in the area and the same day my sister and her husband arrived from their home in Cadiz. We returned to London for the investiture. Our daughter Joan came over from California and so did our friends the Kudernas.

November 2 was the day of the investiture. Megan and Joan were invited to the palace. It was a most impressive ceremony. The British do this kind of thing with great elan. I found the queen a very gracious lady. I was able to tell her that Megan and I had met Prince Charles and Princess Anne in Nairobi. She was pleased.

Fred Hunter, the representative of the *Christian Science Moniter*, met us in Nairobi with a bouquet of flowers for Megan. We were due to leave Kenya in six months so were lookng forward to a busy time. We took over the Duncan home. They were business people who had been there for many years. It was a pleasant estate and again we had three large dogs for companions. They used to stand on their hind legs and eat the avocados, which grow to such a size here. We thought of the small avocados which sold for fifty cents each in California.

Before leaving Kenya we made one of our last trips into the countryside. This was to Lake Nakuru to see the flamingo—surely one of the world's most fascinating animal scenes. We stood on the lakeshore and watched them. There were a million birds along the shores, and in the distance you can see hippos with their snouts above the surface of the lake. Mind where you walk in this area—there are hippo tracks, and dung!

Just before we left AHITI the students were giving a farewell party for Dr. Mann. We were included and were delighted to receive the gifts and thanks of the students. It had all been so worthwhile, and Megan and I were very happy.

The magic of East Africa is difficult to explain. It cannot be put into words. The country and peoples are so varied. There is the beauty of the land, the flowers, the trees, and the wildlife. It captures you and will not let you go. There is such a variety of color, beautiful Indian girls in their *saris,* Sikh men in their turbans, and the occasional half-naked Masai warrior, and so on. I read of someone who was visiting a leper colony in Kenya. It was Christmas and the patients were singing and happy. At the same time came the news on the air that a rich and famous movie star had killed herself. A woman with fame and fortune despaired and here were people with nothing who were singing for joy. It makes one wonder. Our friends in California do not understand why we think that life is safer and happier in many ways in "darkest Africa." We will be back.

We have come a long way, and Megan and I have had a wonderful and interesting life meeting and making friends with people in many countries—people of different colors and creeds. We have lived with Greeks and Turks, Arabs and Jews, and blacks and whites. There are many problems, yes—but there is a unifying force of Divine Love available if only mankind will grasp it.